ebdu

STUPIDITY AND TEARS

STUPIDITY AND TEARS

ALSO BY HERBERT KOHL

The Age of Complexity
36 Children
The Open Classroom
View from the Oak (with Judith Kohl)
Growing with Your Children
Growing Minds: On Becoming a Teacher
From Archetype to Zeitgeist: An Essential Guide to Powerful Ideas
"I Won't Learn from You"
Should We Burn Babar?
The Discipline of Hope

Stupidity and Tears

Teaching and Learning in Troubled Times

Herbert Kohl

THE NEW PRESS

NEW YORK
LONDON

Published in the United States by The New Press, New York, 2003
Distributed by W. W. Norton & Company, Inc., New York

LIBRARY OF CONGRESS CATALOGING-IN-PUBLICATION DATA
Kohl, Herbert R.
Stupidity and tears : teaching and learning
in troubled times/Herbert Kohl.
p.   cm.
ISBN 1-56584-851-9 (hc)
1. Teaching. 2. Learning. 3. Education—United States.
4. Kohl, Herbert R. I. Title: Stupidity and tears. II. Title.
LB1025.3.K66 2004
371.102—dc21   2003044204

The New Press was established in 1990 as a not-for-profit alternative
to the large, commercial publishing houses currently dominating
the book publishing industry. The New Press operates in the public interest
rather than for private gain, and is committed to publishing,
in innovative ways, works of educational, cultural, and community value
that are often deemed insufficiently profitable.

The New Press
38 Greene Street, 4th floor
New York, NY 10013
www.thenewpress.com

In the United Kingdom:
6 Salem Road
London W2 4BU

Composition by dix!

Printed in the United States of America

2   4   6   8   10   9   7   5   3   1

TO MY COURAGEOUS STUDENTS AT THE UNIVERSITY
OF SAN FRANCISCO, WHO ARE COMMITTED TO TEACHING
WELL DURING HARD TIMES, AND TO MIKE SAHAKIAN,
WHO NURTURES ME AND ALL OUR STUDENTS

Contents

Preface and Acknowledgments   *xi*

Part I: The Tears   *1*
1. Stupidity and Tears   3
2. Worrying: Notes Toward a Moral Education
   Curriculum Post–9/11   39

Part II: The Joy   *69*
3. Write It in the Sky:
   Imagining the World Otherwise   71
4. Topsy-Turvies: Teacher Talk and Student Talk   101

*Part III: Educational Reflections on Becoming
   Sixty-five*   *119*
5. Burning Out and Flaring Up   121

Appendix: Developing Teachers for Social Justice   *139*
Notes   *159*

Preface and Acknowledgments

The essays in this book are about sustaining the joy of teaching while under pressure. Facing budget cuts, cynical politicians, and right-wing pressures to dismantle public education, many teachers, both veteran and new to the calling, are staying the course and learning to provide quality education for poor children. Their pains and joys are not present in papers on educational research, nor is there much encouragement for their efforts on the part of the educational establishment. In this book I want to share something of their lives, their problems, and their joys. I also hope to share my own reflections on teaching and struggling over the past forty years for the development of quality education for the least-served children in our society. At sixty-five, I have more energy, spend more time, and feel more pain and joy when it comes to teaching and learning than I ever have.

A number of people have helped me make this book possible. First of all, and as always, I want to thank my wife, Judy, who has shared this long journey and has always been there in times of joy and despair. I also want to thank my editor, Diane Wachtell, whose tough comments always help me hone my work. It is a pleasure to work with her. Other people who have helped are Paul Warren, former Dean of the School of Education at the University of San Francisco, who made my work there possible; my students Francis Blanchette and Andy Terranova, who read parts of the manuscript and provided very useful comments; the people I have worked with at Mission High School and Sanchez Elementary School in San Francisco; and my agent and friend Wendy Weil, who always supports my work.

STUPIDITY AND TEARS

Part I

The Tears

1.
Stupidity and Tears

Against stupidity the very gods
Themselves contend in vain[1]
> —Friedrich von Schiller,
> *Joan of Arc,* act 3, scene 5

In 1937, Robert Musil, the author of *A Man Without Qualities,* gave a lecture in Vienna titled "On Stupidity." He began by asserting

> Anyone who presumes to speak about stupidity today runs the risk of coming to grief in a number of ways. It may be interpreted as insolence on his part; it may even be interpreted as disturbing the progress of our time. . . . And so a question gradually arises that refuses to be put off: Just what is stupidity?

Musil wrote this at a troubling, tragic, and stupid moment in European history, in the midst of the spread of Nazism. Now, in the early twenty-first century, we are also in troubling, tragic, and stupid times, and the issue of stupidity and its relationship to how people think and react to complex personal, social, and economic challenges is as important as it was in the late thirties. However, given the scope of the problem, I decided to focus on a field I know and have worked in for over forty years—education—and try to understand the ways in which educational policies and theories about young people, learning, schooling, and public education are stupid and have the consequence of perpetuating ignorance, keeping poor, defiant, and marginalized youth "in their place." In addition, I want to concentrate on how systems apply pressure on idealistic and creative teachers to make them act stupidly and perform in the classroom in ways that are opposed to their conscience, knowledge, and experience.

I have encountered stupidity in education many times over the years. One particular story stands out. Les Blanc and Maureen Gosling are documentary filmmakers whose works—including *Chulas Fronteras, The Blues According to Lightnin' Hopkins,* and *Garlic Is as Good as Ten Mothers*—celebrate music, family, community, and cooking. When my children were in elementary and junior high school in Point Arena, California, Les sent me a copy of one of his films, *Always for Pleasure.* The film takes place in New Orleans before and during Mardi Gras. It's about Louisiana food, the black Indian societies who march in the Mardi Gras parade, and the way in which the run-up to Mardi Gras affects community, family, and culture. The center of the film is the march across New Orleans of the Wild Magnolias and the Wild Chapatulas—two of the black societies—all decked out in flowers and feathers, wearing carnival costumes made to celebrate American Indian tribal dress at its most elegant and elaborate. It culminates in a dance and song contest between the "tribes."

I found the film delightful, an energetic multicultural celebration of life, and convinced the principal of my kids' school to show the film to a student assembly. My children and their friends loved the film, and I went home feeling I had made a small but not insignificant contribution toward bringing multi-cultural education to the school. After dinner, the phone calls began. One friend called and said she had heard that I had shown a picture at the school that had sexual "exposure" in it. A stranger called accusing me of being immoral, forcing porno-graphic films on children, and engaging in corruption of the youth. A third caller swore that I would never be able to set foot in the school again after they (who?) got done with me.

The next day I discovered that a group of community members had circulated a petition demanding that I be pub-licly censured and prevented from ever entering the school, even to pick up my own children. One hundred and fifty-seven people signed it (I still have a copy). It took watching the film two or three times for me to figure out what the problem was. About two thirds of the way through the film, as the tribes are marching toward each other, is a 2.3-second flash of an African American man cutting across the path of the march. Attached to his belt is a five-foot-long purple sock dragging along the ground. That was the exposure.

I thought it would be easy to neutralize the situation by going to the originators of the petition and asking them what they saw in the film and how the whole exposure-fantasy devel-oped. As it turned out, not one person who had signed the pe-tition had seen the film. Worse, they didn't want to see it because they thought it contained pornography. I had come di-rectly against a wall of stupidity. They would not look on what they had not seen, but went ahead with the petition anyway.

Finally I asked Les Blanc to send me a film clip of the of-fending moment and put it on a loop so I could show it over and over. The night the petition was presented to the school board, I came armed with a projector and the clip and insisted that the board watch it before they acted. Many of the people who had presented the petition left the room in protest before I showed the "obscene" moment. The board members, most of whom were tired after a full day's work, let me show the clip but missed the 2.3 seconds the first time it ran, so I showed the loop over and over until, very slowly, one and then the rest of them started to laugh. The chair said, "Issue closed," and I continued my volunteer work at the school. The fundamentalist Christian community that engineered the petition, though it retreated on this issue, continues almost twenty years later in its efforts to suppress free expression, censor textbooks, and keep biological theory under theological control. Fortunately, in Point Arena, community demographics have changed, and their efforts are not taken too seriously anymore.

This was not the first time I had encountered willful stupidity. Years before, about 1969, when I co-directed an alternative high school in Berkeley, our theater troupe traveled to Claremont, California, to perform at a reading conference. While there, I encountered another example of people making the conscious choice to manipulate ignorance as a way of asserting power and concealing social, political, and personal agendas. Our students and staff were put up at a motel near the college. When we arrived, it was about ninety degrees, and the students decided to take a swim in the motel's pool. We had a meeting with the kids and made it clear that there was to be no naked swimming or guerrilla theater in the pool. Everyone wore a proper swimsuit and was polite to the other guests at the pool. Our staff were deployed about the pool to be sure that the kids were respectful, since some of them were capable of doing crazy things. It was the summer of People's Park in Berkeley, and many of the students used to tease the police by running naked through fire hydrants they had turned on.

Our students went swimming and I was with them, sitting on the edge of the pool, chatting with other guests and explaining how wonderful it was that our students were invited to a

6

college conference. The kids were great, and it was a pleasure to watch them have fun and not be worried, for a short time, about the tension and conflict they were facing in the political climate of Berkeley in 1969.

After about half an hour, the motel manger called me into his office and ordered me to get all of my naked students out of the pool. My students were in the pool, but the only naked person there was a baby unrelated to us in the wading area. I told the manager that we were very careful to be sure that every student was properly dressed and asked him to come out to the pool and see for himself. He refused, stating in a seething and hostile voice, "I will not look upon such obscene nakedness. Get them out of there."

No matter how I tried, he stood his ground and threatened to evict us from the motel. I said his response was stupid and that all he had to do was come out and look at the kids. Finally I gave up and told the kids they had to get out of the pool and begin rehearsing for the evening performance since I couldn't figure out how to deal with being evicted from the motel.

That evening I complained to our hosts about the stupidity of the situation, and the conference director took me aside and said it was stupid but it was also willful. He had received a call from the manager that day complaining that black students and white students were swimming together in his pool, and that that would chase away his other guests. He was willfully stupid to me in order to mask his naked pragmatic racism. I didn't know whether to scream or cry.

However, the relationship between stupidity and tears is more complex than I imagined then, since I had not thought of myself as stupid or thought about good people who consciously force themselves to become stupid and agonize over the consequences. Last spring I met with a young and gifted teacher who has let me do theater with her fourth and fifth graders once a week. Rosa's students are bold, willing to try just about any experiment with, as we call it, *tragedia* and *commedia*. Their ensemble work is imaginative, intelligent, and spiced by a wicked but not hostile desire to test the limits of propriety and use the stage to parody and mock the adult world.

My meeting with Rosa had to do with the children and her conflicts as their teacher. She is a bilingual-education teacher, and all of these children are blessed and punished for knowing and speaking more than one language and being more comfortable in their home language, Spanish, than in the English they are clearly acquiring. It was a few days after testing time. She had been forced by the San Francisco Unified School District and the State of California to test her students in English only. Not only that, she had to give instructions in English and couldn't answer students' questions in Spanish even if they had to do with how to go about taking the test. She had to become a tender of the testing machine and put aside both her compassion for the children and her knowledge of what they knew and how intelligent they were. She also had to find a way to ignore her moral depression over imposing tasks on her students that both she and they knew they could not perform.

Rosa knew that she was complicit in setting her students up for failure, and it was tearing her apart. She is a dedicated teacher, a lifer, and it went against her heart and mind as an educator to be forced into being an instrument of her students' humiliation. Almost in tears, she said, "I have never felt so stupid in my whole life."

She felt stupid because of the kind of stupidity she was forced to perpetuate. English-only testing of these children was not merely cruel and unfair, it made no human or pedagogical sense. It led to no benefit for any child. The students' scores wouldn't help her teach any better, nor would they help other educators design programs that would be effective for her students. The tests were imposed on the children because certain wealthy, conservative Californians were able, through the initiative process, to impose state-mandated school policies that effectively prohibited the use of Spanish in the schools. Rosa was the agent of this stupid idea that cut children off from their home language and promised to provide them with a permanent disadvantage, a position that was laughable and led to tears at the same time.

Rosa is bilingual. She knows how to develop Spanish-speaking youngsters into fully functioning, academically successful bilingual citizens. However, she has been forced to become stupid in order to keep her job. She has to deny what she knows, pretend to supervisors that she is abiding by the foolish English-only mandates, and sneak her sound pedagogy into the stupid and demeaning programs being imposed upon her. I know she will not give up on the children, and so, ironically, the theater I've been working on with her class has become her mode, too. Parody, mock conformity, anything to protect the children as they become fully bilingual learners. These strategies of inauthentic conformity complicate her teaching life. The stupidity game is painful to play, but more and more teachers who are forced to teach against their conscience and pedagogical experience are playing it because they do not want to give up on their students.

This was Rosa's first year in a situation like this. However, I know many teachers who, the third or fourth time through the process, stop worrying about it and simply accept part of their teaching lives as stupid. They develop a cynical attitude toward their profession while trying to maintain their love of teaching. One of them recently told me that teaching in California has become a stupid job, one in which both common sense and good pedagogy are replaced by state mandates and politicians' programs. Living with stupidity alienates teachers from their work and is perhaps one of the main causes of teacher turnover among people who love children and find teaching magical. It is certainly what motivates many young and gifted teachers, who want to teach in the most underserved public schools, to migrate to charter schools and private schools and to open their minds to working in voucher-based programs, or to leave the profession altogether. Many intelligent and caring teachers simply do not want to pay the price of making themselves stupid as the cost of teaching in public schools.

I first encountered the idea that stupidity was a form of learned social behavior subject to sociological analysis in an essay by the anthropologist Jules Henry published in 1968 in the *New York Review of Books* entitled "Education for Stupidity." Henry argued that people are not born stupid but can be educated, seduced, forced, or tricked into stupidity. For him, creating stupidity in education has a social purpose. Keeping *some* people stupid is a conscious strategy that prevents them from understanding why they are required to act against their conscience and counter to their intelligence. Stupidity, in Henry's sense, has nothing to do with intelligence. He says he wrote the essay

> to illustrate the development of legitimate social stupidity in elementary and high schools in the United States. There is always a question of how much information the members of any culture may be permitted to have; and throughout history it has been assumed that most of the population should be kept ignorant. . . . [T]he world is presented to children and adolescents in such a way as to prevent them from getting from school the information necessary to enable them to form an intelligent opinion about the world.[2]

Jules Henry's focus was on students, but what about teachers? Are there ways in which creating stupid teachers perpetuates stupidity in the classroom and keeps stupid systems of education functioning? This question easily can be taken as an insult by teachers, but it is meant in an entirely different spirit. The question is whether making teachers act as if they are stupid serves current public educational systems well: Are teachers who do not question, who do not have educational philosophies or critical perspectives on their work, and who do not have time or tools to think through the nature and consequences of their pedagogy precisely the most desired of employees? And does resistance to stupidity become a form of insurrection or self-destruction?

It is essential to distinguish between stupidity in the context of this essay and some more usual uses of the word "stupid." Stupidity that leads to tears is not a matter of people lacking intelligence, or making clumsy or thoughtless decisions, or acting in ways that make them the butt of jokes. It is not a matter of ignorance. Rather, it is a form of institutional and social coercion that traps people into acting in ways they consider to be stupid and, in the context of teaching, counter to the work they feel they must do to help their students. It can be a form of humiliation similar to that which many students feel in school when they are ridiculed for trying to get the right answer and failing to give the teacher exactly what he or she wants. Or it can be a form of confinement to insane norms of educational programs that restrict creativity and clearly have not worked. Becoming stupid can be demoralizing. But it can also be a call to resistance and the rebirth of teacher militancy.

I first became aware of stupidity and tears when I was in high school. In 1953, I was a delegate from the Bronx High School of Science to the American Legion's Empire Boys State. The four-day retreat was designed as a simulation of a political convention for a national election and included nominating a presidential and vice presidential candidate, choosing candidates for statewide officers, developing a party campaign structure, and drawing up and adopting a party platform. It was supposed to be an exercise in democratic leadership for high school student council leaders.

The first two days were exciting. I was interested in helping draw up the platform and, given that we were in the midst of the McCarthy and HUAC era, I hoped to introduce some statements defending First and Fifth Amendments' rights and opposing the intimidation of people because of their political views. At Bronx Science it was impossible to avoid these issues, since many of our teachers were fired for taking the Fifth Amendment or refusing to testify before HUAC. I also wanted to deal with racism in the high schools, which was an issue before the New York City Inter-GO organization, where I was a representative.

However, on the second day of committee meetings I was taken aside by one of our American Legion instructors and told that my proposals, as important as they were, didn't fit the format of the convention, which was supposed to focus on student issues. I maintained that rights and racism were student issues, but all of the other students on the committee fell into line and accepted the argument that high school students didn't know enough to take stands on "adult" issues; the platform ended up dealing with rights to plan dances, control student council budgets, and develop grievance procedures within the school. They accepted being infantilized and neutralized by adult political handlers.

The rest of the retreat unfolded as a wheeling, dealing popularity contest, with Upstate New York united against the City,

and well-organized, upper-middle-class students who had arrived at the convention with working political machines out-
witting New York City students who had not known one
another before and had not been prepped by their local American Legion chapters on how to "take" a convention. (In my
community there were union committees and Workingman's
Circle committees, but I had never encountered the American
Legion or one of the legionnaires.)

As the legion's scenario unfolded, I was accused of not entering the spirit of the game. I wasn't alone, and a small caucus
of resisters developed. However, the system had no place for us
since the goal was to adopt one platform with one set of candidates and to do it with a minimum of controversy. We were to
mime politics and participate in a charade that was no different
from the power-and-popularity politics of adult America.

The final event was the actual convention, in which candidates were chosen and platforms approved. American flags,
horns, whistles, and confetti were distributed. Cheerleaders
were chosen to orchestrate the final event, which was loud with
horns blaring, whistles blowing, confetti and streamers flying,
and shouting and cheering. There was nothing to choose from,
no debate, no contestation of ideas and values. The Upstate
crowd won, as it was set up to do. I found myself standing
alone, almost crying, feeling very much the way the young
teacher Rosa must have felt confronting her testing nightmare.
I couldn't experience the joy others obviously took from being
part of the event. I felt lonely and excluded. The whole thing
seemed stupid to me—how could people cheer on command,
act engaged, and allow themselves to be manipulated to please
the American Legion's sense of democracy as a popularity
contest? And yet I wondered about myself. Was *I* the one who
was stupid for not joining in and doing what I enjoyed doing at
basketball games? Was I stupid for worrying about issues and

ideas when the mock convention was just theater, not meant to change the world?

I remember coming home to the Bronx confused and depressed. Were they stupid, was I stupid? I had no sociological or psychological language to describe my dilemma. When I returned home I told my father that I thought the whole thing was stupid. In his usual way, he said I was the stupid one—stupid not to know that they were stupid or know how to deal with the pressures to act in ways that oppose your beliefs.

This was my first real encounter with an effort to manipulate my will in an obvious and planned manner. Whether I was enthusiastic or not, whether I wanted to cheer and throw confetti or not, I was expected to conform. That was the rule of the game. I felt some guilt at not being willing to play the game but also felt an inner conviction that I couldn't play it. And I was punished for standing outside of the game by being a pariah at the end of the meetings, avoided by all of the "winners." They loved the game and made it difficult for people who resisted the rituals of conformity that had rewarded them. In retrospect I see this as the beginning of a personal awareness of issues of conscience.

Many people throughout the world face similar issues of conscience on a life-threatening level. Whether to act and get into trouble while maintaining self-respect, or conform and feel stupid—this is a major struggle for thinking people.

In the summer of 1998, a year before my father died, he insisted upon referring to himself as stupid. It was his favorite lament at the end of his life. No matter what I would say, he summed up his ninety years as a futile exercise in complicity. Of course he wasn't stupid, just bitter. His attitude toward life was summed up by a Sam Goldwyn quote: "You've got to take the bitter with the sour."

I understand this Yiddish sense of life as a travail to endure and mock. But my father's feelings about his own stupidity remain troubling to me. As we talked during his last three or four months, his philosophy of stupidity emerged and has affected my thinking about how values can be eroded and self-respect compromised, destroyed, or distorted when people succumb to their feelings of vulnerability. He told me he was stupid because of decisions he had made against his own better judgment, because of fear, family pressure, lack of understanding the ways of strangers, and governmental pressure. He also thought he was stupid because of trusting people too much, of worrying about doing the right thing and, most of all, abandoning his childhood dreams and compromising his moral principles.

My father was not stupid in the sense of dumb, thick, dense, slow, dull, or obtuse. He also did not do stupid things. His words and troubled reflections embody the original definition of the word "stupidity," which, according to the etymologist Eric Partridge, comes from the Indo European–Sanskrit *stupere*: to be knocked stupid or insensible, to be numbed or astonished. The world he lived and worked in stupefied him, and he had no confidence in his own actions or decisions.

He attended New York City public school and told me how he'd decided to hide the lunch his mother prepared for him since it had garlic, kosher salami, and pickles. His teachers and many of the other kids who were assimilating Jews, Irish, and Italians laughed at him and several of his teachers told him to clean his mouth out before he came to class because he reeked of poverty and garlic, so he decided to bypass lunch. The teachers also kept calling him to the office and having the nurse examine him for lice before allowing him to return to class. My father's experiences, which I always believed he exaggerated, became plain truths when I came upon this quote from a 1939 issue of *Life* magazine praising the baseball player Joe DiMaggio:

> Although he learned Italian first, Joe, now 24, speaks English without an accent, and is otherwise adapted to most US mores. Instead of olive oil or smelly bear grease he keeps his hair slick with water. He never reeks of garlic and prefers chicken chow mein to spaghetti.[3]

The idea that chicken chow mein is more American than spaghetti is just another example of what stupefied my father. Reflecting upon my father's comments and my own experiences trying to transform public education, I have concluded that intelligent, painful, and tearful stupidity has four components:

* *It implies acting in a way that you consciously understand to be against your principles and that makes you feel foolish to yourself no matter how other people perceive or judge you.*

* *It means consciously acting stupidly as a form of resistance to being called stupid and has the effect of learning to take control of your own image as stupid, including elements of theater that reveal you are aware of acting against your conscience, and an ironic stance toward one's own life, often expressed through self-deprecating humor.*

* *It opens you to ridicule and discovery and therefore makes it difficult to trust others.*

* *Finally, at its most redeeming, it allows you to perceive the stupidity in others and feel part of a silent conspiracy that still honors authenticity, while betraying it.*

I know many students and teachers whose feelings about their school lives involve awareness of stupidity and tears. They feel they are forced to act stupidly, which is not the same as being stupid. These are not people who are bitter about life itself or generalize their school experience to an indictment of their whole lives, as my father did. In fact, the things they do outside of school often resist the stupidity of what they felt forced to do during school time.

I learned about what "school time" meant when I first began teaching in 1961. In my first class there were students drumming on their desks, putting their heads down and pretending to be asleep, falling off chairs, and tripping or falling down on the way to get a book or piece of paper. I initially thought the kids were clowning around or defying me, and as a young teacher I figured it would be easy to overcome most of that dysfunctional behavior. It wasn't, and I still observe its current manifestations forty years later. One of the most striking things that happened to me in my whole career as an educator—and has influenced my thinking about young people and schools for years—happened in that fifth-grade class in P.S. 107 in Manhattan. Three of my students, Antonio, Hugh, and Luis, were experts at falling off their chairs whenever I tried to teach anything. Two others, Tamisa and Haydee, were great at screaming and shouting about other kids, and insulting me when they were expected to do any work.

It all puzzled me. I didn't know any of the kids, and hadn't said or done anything to anger them. Their stupid behavior (stupid because it prevented them from learning) began the day I arrived in January to take over from a series of substitute teachers who had given up on them. For the first three or four weeks of teaching I felt at war with my students' resistance to learning. I watched them on the playground and saw them playing with one another without fighting or craziness. I decided to have lunch in the school cafeteria with my students and found them perfectly civil, often funny and delightful. But as soon as we hit the classroom after lunch, there they were doing stupid things again.

As an educator I was saved by my conception of the students' behavior as stupid and dysfunctional rather than defiant or manifesting their incapacity to learn. Before getting my public school credential I taught for six months in a private school for schizophrenic and autistic children, and therefore knew perfectly well that my current students were not severely disturbed. They had control over their behavior and had somehow learned that acting stupid forced teachers to leave them alone when it came to learning. They had learned not to learn and had figured out that it cost them less, humanly, to pretend to be stupid than to become failures in a system that didn't support their learning.

I wondered what they felt about their own stupid behavior and got some insight into their thinking about their behavior when I got to know Antonio and Luis and their family on a personal level. One day after school Antonio and Luis asked if I would have dinner at Luis's house one night. Their parents wanted to meet me because the boys had told them about the time we spent before and after school. They also told me they were cousins—a fact I had not learned from their school records, though it was clear that they were a dynamic duo in class when they wanted to make trouble.

I accepted, and brought with me some books for the kids and some flowers for their parents. It was a privilege to be invited into their lives, and I was curious about these kids who could be so focused and lovely in one context and so crazy in another. Luis's family's apartment was on the top floor of a five-story walk-up on a very rough block. When I entered the apartment I was overwhelmed by the glorious smell of Puerto Rican cooking at its best: roast pork, *bacalao, pastelles,* plantains, greens, and other dishes. Luis and Antonio were there, as were their brothers, sisters, and parents. I was an honored guest at a banquet.

The boys were gracious, polite, dressed for church, and became, along with Luis's older sister Maria, my translators. Everyone except Antonio's father spoke Spanish. The evening was full of stories about their family's lives in Puerto Rico, about fishing off the south coast of the island and coming to New York, about serving in the U.S. Army during World War II, and also about my grandparents who raised me and were immigrants from Eastern Europe. They wanted to know as much about me as I wanted to know about them.

When I got home I realized that Luis and Antonio had become invisible translators as the evening went on and we sat around talking about our lives and experiences. No drumming, no falling off chairs, nothing but an occasional and respectful question.

Antonio's father, Alfredo, told me before I left that I should call him if the boys did anything wrong in class, while thanking me for helping them so much. He had noticed they spent time with books and read to him, the only English-speaking adult in the family. He saw their progress and wanted me to know that he backed what I was doing.

But whatever learning was taking place was not in the classroom. I stayed up most of the night after that dinner, confounded at the disconnect between my students' behavior in school and at home. I was particularly struck by the way Luis had participated in the adult conversation and by the ease with which he moved from English to Spanish. Dual images of Luis and Antonio flashed back and forth in my mind. That dinner had a profound effect on my thinking about my students and about schooling. My challenge was to discover a way to get them to function at school as they had functioned at home.

When I expressed my concerns to Antonio's father a few days later, he suggested a mechanism of control for the boys: he said he'd beat them if they misbehaved. But that's not what I wanted. I would rather put up with some more of their stupid institutional behavior until I figured out how to make a classroom where the students would have no reason or desire to be stupid or defiant.

Another time, Luis, his older sister Maria, and I were having a conversation in the living room of their home after we'd all had dinner. Maria is a brilliant, compassionate person, and Luis trusted and looked up to her. During the conversation Maria wanted to know how Luis was behaving in class, and I told her the truth. I also said I knew he was too smart to act so stupidly. Maria turned to Luis and asked him what he thought about his behavior, and he burst into tears. He said he had to do it, that most other teachers he knew thought he was stupid and insulted him, so he'd decided to act stupid but in a way that threatened them and got them off his back. Also, his friends acted that way, and if he separated himself from the other guys, they'd look on him as a chump. He felt trapped in a system and didn't know a way out of stupidity. What he did make clear to me was that he did not want to act stupidly and knew he wasn't stupid. He needed strategies and support to "un-stupid" himself.

As the semester developed, I decided to come to class early and stay late so I could prepare my classroom and create an environment where the students felt comfortable enough to give up their dysfunctional stupidity. Antonio, Hugh, Luis, and Haydee appeared at the classroom door before I did, no matter how early I showed up. Nor did it matter whether the custodian had unlocked the doors. They knew how to get in and out of the school at will and never, in all the time we spent together, told me how they did it.

The four of them made it clear that they came to school early for two reasons: to help me clean up the classroom and ready it for the day, and, most surprising, so that I could teach them how to read. Eventually I arrived even earlier so that we could both clean the classroom and do individualized reading. They were all superb students. My speculation was that as we forged a trusting relation they would stop being so crazy and stupid during the school day and would become peer tutors who would help change the classroom culture into one in which learning could be both serious and fun. I was wrong. They were wonderful until 8:40, when the other students arrived. From then until the end of the day, when they stayed behind to help me clean, they periodically burst into drumming and chair falling. But the conviction wasn't there. They did enough to save face with their peers, but I began to get the feeling that they didn't want to push things to the point where I would no longer be there for them before and after school.

I didn't figure out how to eliminate dysfunctional stupidity from my classroom during my first semester teaching, but I did learn that their behavior, which was meant to drive me out of the classroom, was also a source of grief to them. As the school year ended I managed to get assigned to a class that would have the four of them and several of my other students the next year, and decided to redesign my classroom and approach to teaching over the summer. But it never happened—I was involuntarily transferred to another, more "difficult" school during August for "excessive socializing" with my students and raising impertinent questions at faculty meetings. My evaluation during that first semester as a public school teacher rated me unsatisfactory for being too close to the students and their parents.

Reflecting upon the situation at the end of that first semester of teaching, I concluded that it was the school that was stupid, not the students. They did not want to act the way they did in school; did not act that way at home or on the streets. Stupidity was their school mode of functioning, and unfortunately they themselves were the major victims of this clever act of theater. I also realized that they were close to tears about their own behavior, no matter how much they might boast about how they'd upset a teacher or gotten away with something. There were deep contradictions in their behavior, and they were vulnerable—vulnerable in ways I hoped could lead them toward learning and away from stupidity. This is not much different from the way many teachers feel about their own institutionally enforced behavior these days.

I still see schoolchildren doing the kinds of things that Antonio and Luis did over forty years ago. The cultivated stupidity they manifest in class today is no different, though sometimes it is more baroque, adding extemporaneous rap and break-dancing steps to the usual drumming and sleeping. The students face the same cynical forms of schooling and react in the same ways. They are trapped in a system that claims to have their learning and success in mind, though really it is designed and administered as a failure system with high-stakes testing, "teacher-proof" curriculum, unrealizable standards, and punishment for so-called underperforming schools that serve the children of the poor and working class. And the continual threat of being called a failure from the time they are as young as four or five drives many children to do crazy and stupid things. As one high school student, Reginald, said to me recently, "I'd rather

be defiant and stupid in class than let the teacher call me a failure. My friends know I'm not dumb, and we laugh at the
teacher together."

Later he elaborated on his frustrations with himself in
school. He wanted to learn, couldn't get a handle on what his
teachers expected of him, had a few bad years in middle
school, and simply could not stand the idea that he wasn't
smart enough to make it in school. Since he didn't know how to
succeed, he decided he would rather play at being stupid. He
would let "them" forget about his mind and pay attention to his
behavior. At least, he said, "it kept me from giving up." He did
give up trying in school, though, in order to escape from failure, since there was no support for his learning. At the end of
the conversation he was as close to tears as such a strong and
proud young man allowed himself to be outside of family and
intimate friends. Unfortunately, Reginald's behavior ended up
hurting him. The tension between willful stupidity and failure
leaves no room for the student to win.

The distinction between failing in school and behaving
stupidly in order to avoid failing is not often discussed by educators. However, we have to develop strategies for helping students get beyond their terror of failing and of being classified
as incapable of learning. This is becoming increasingly difficult as teachers are finding themselves in the same situation as
their students. They are being forced to drive the failure system
by conforming to regulated and controlled demands from administrators, the state and federal governments, and local
politicians. For example, many public school districts these
days have adopted a single curriculum tied into an expensive,
so-called teacher-proof program such as Open Court or Success for All. These programs come with a script for teachers to
follow, lesson-by-lesson and day-by-day. The rationale of these
programs is that districts that serve the children of the poor are

so badly organized, some form of instructional alignment must be used to achieve uniformity and standards within entire districts that have histories of being dysfunctional. They are intended to ensure that even the worst teachers will be able to deliver adequate learning.

That goal is admirable though foolish, since a terrible teacher will be terrible with whatever he or she is required to do. In addition, there is little evidence that the programs do or even can achieve what they claim. It is an attempt to take the "human factor" out of teaching, when that factor is at the heart of all good teaching. What they do achieve is demoralizing successful teachers and new teachers who come to teaching with a desire to be creative and helpful to students. Teacher-proofing education is an insult to teachers, as it assumes they are stupid and forces them to act as if they were stupid. It denies their will and creativity in the service of putting order into a system that often borders on the chaotic. Certainly the systems need coherence and standards, but it is very unlikely that one can succeed in transforming a system by making the people charged with that transformation into robots who feel stupid and resentful about their work.

Recently I had a student in the teacher-credential program I direct who is an excellent teacher in a difficult school. Roger's students do extremely well in class and are very creative. They also score well on high-stakes tests. He has recently been ordered by supervisors from the central district office to give up his thoughtful, imaginative, and effective practice in order to conform to mandates to follow the script of Open Court. Though he protested that his students were already achieving beyond the district's expectations, he was told he had to fall in line.

What happens when you are ordered to undo good practice and become an automaton? Roger loves his students, and doesn't want to be defiant or lose his job. The only option, he said, was to act stupid and be subversive at the same time. For a while he pretended to comply while preserving the creative and most motivating parts of his curriculum. But the administration was adamant. He had to follow the script, like it or not, and he had to endure what he called the "Open Court police," former district curriculum supervisors assigned to monitor compliance. Going to school every day went from being a joy to being a nightmare. He told me he got through the whole thing by pretending he was on stage, though when holding the script in his hand he saw how to help a child by throwing the script out, he felt like screaming or crying. Eventually he decided that stupidity wasn't worth the sacrifice of his students' learning and he remained subversive for the rest of the academic year. He took a stand against stupidity, but also took a leave of absence for the next year to look into other, more creative, teaching options, and it is open to question whether he'll return to the district or the community whose children he served so well.

Roger, Rosa, and Reginald all acted in ways that were consciously against their principles and beliefs and that made them look foolish to themselves. They didn't act with evil intent, and they knew what they were doing was theater. All three complied and tried to show other people that they were what they were supposed to be—in the case of Roger and Rosa, compliant and stupid teachers, and in the case of Reginald, a stupid kid. None of them, however, learned how to take advantage of their stance toward their school lives; it left them feeling weak, powerless, frustrated, angry, and just about in tears.

Acting stupid or conforming to stupid functioning made all three keenly aware that they were open to ridicule from their friends or peers, and made them a bit paranoid at school. They always had to worry about being discovered to be shams. This made it hard to trust others unless they were co-conspirators and in on the pretense.

Finally, it made them keenly aware of the stupidity of others and of the system in which they were trapped. This consciousness made them, in different ways, feel part of a silent conspiracy to preserve good teaching under pressure. The teachers did not give up their love of teaching and their belief in the capabilities and intelligence of their students. And Reginald is planning to leave high school, get a job, and attend junior college. They did not generalize stupidity into a philosophy of life. They all have rich and interesting lives outside of school. But they all came to consider school to be that part of their lives where being stupid was normal behavior.

Manufacturing stupidity in education has an institutional component. People often get forced into being stupid because there are legal and infrastructural constraints on the systems in which they work that force them to function against their conscience or counter to their experience and knowledge. I remember working with the Chicano Student Union at one of the colleges in the University of California system. Together we planned a summer literacy program utilizing undergraduates, several teachers, and some community activists. We had the support of the local school district and the university and were funded under Title I of the Elementary and Secondary Education Act of 1965.

The act signaled a major commitment by the federal government to provide funds for the education of the poor with an emphasis on African American and other minority children. Title I of the act provided funds specially designated for direct funding to schools for specific children who performed poorly in school and had backgrounds of poverty.

The summer program worked well. Students attended and loved being around the college kids. Community people volunteered to provide resources, and parents came at all hours helping out, working with small groups of children, and learning from the teachers how to help their own children at home. The teachers and college students were excited by their work, and by the end of the summer we had succeeded in raising most of the students' scores to grade level. Everyone agreed that the program should continue during the school year, and we all anticipated that the district would be delighted with our students' test scores. You might say that the program worked in a stupidity-free zone. We acted according to knowledge and conviction, had the freedom to develop the program, and accepted responsibility for the results of our work.

Two weeks before school began, the program coordinators were called into the district office and were told that the program could not be continued during the school year since it no longer qualified for Title I funds. It seemed that federal funding was restricted to programs that served children who were not performing up to grade level. Our success meant defunding. I remember being stupefied by the decision.

The program coordinators were fired, the community volunteers were sent home, the parents were no longer encouraged to volunteer, and the children returned to the system that had failed them in the first place. The bureaucrats, in order to keep Title I money, had to keep the children below grade level. The assistant superintendent told me she felt the whole situation was crazy but that she had no control over it. Stupidity and tears all over again. This time, however, it was not the teachers or the students who were forced to act in stupid and tearful ways. Rather, it was a thoughtless system with built-in failure. It reminds me of current welfare reform programs where people get cut off after five years and are required to work at jobs that can't possibly support their families—stupidity in the legislation leading to tears on the ground. Even the most caring welfare workers are forced to act against their conscience, and frequently feel the pain of the dysfunctional work they are forced to do, which of course is not as substantial as the pain of their clients.

Ironically, the school district we worked in did succeed in retaining Title I funds, since the students' gains during the summer were lost during the school year, and once again they qualified for funding as failures. The next summer the district went to the university and asked it to renew the summer program with some of the same children who had become requalified for Title I during the school year.

This no longer happens. With the recent reauthorization of the Elementary and Secondary Education Act, we now reward successful programs and punish failed programs. In other words, now if you are already a success with poor children, you get money; and if you are struggling, you get money taken away. The failure system plays its stupid games in many forms.

The maintenance of stupidity is based on the ability to make ignorance normal. In many circumstances, making people stupid is a way of making them conform to other agendas that are often not explicit and are neither rational nor reasonable. In education it is easy to see and hard to undo, since resistance to stupidity often implies confrontation with the system it benefits.

There are traditional tales that remind people of what happens when stupidity becomes normalized. In British folklore there is the town of Gotham, where everyone is a fool and stupidity rules. In Yiddish folklore there is a similar town, Chelm, where everyone is a fool and the leaders are the biggest fools of all. Here is a version of an old tale that I adapted to represent some of the stories teachers tell me of their lives in schools these days.

It seems that there was a steep hill in the middle of Chelm, and children were always falling down the hill and hurting themselves. The hill was the only place in town where children could play, yet it was so dangerous that many children broke their arms and legs and even skulls in falls. The people of Chelm couldn't figure out what to do, so they called in the wise men who, after deliberating for several weeks, came up with the following solutions:

1. Proclaim, as town goals, the elimination of all injuries some time in the distant future.
2. Let the town know that their leaders frown upon carelessness and don't tolerate falling.
3. Advise parents to get tough and keep their children indoors.
4. Inform the children that if they got hurt it was due to their own choice, and part of life in a free community.
5. Build a hospital at the bottom of the hill for those injured children whose parents could afford to pay for medical care.

The community accepted these solutions, and the newspapers proclaimed the wisdom of the town's leadership.

Of course the wise men ignored the children's need to play, failed to prevent injuries, and encouraged no community initiatives to transform the environment in the service of the children.

This story came to mind when the following headline appeared on the front page of the *New York Times* (8/23/02):

With New Rules and
Higher Pay New York Gets
Certified Teachers

The article begins:

> After years of struggling to recruit enough certified teachers to fill
> even half of its classroom vacancies, New York City has attracted
> more than 8,000 qualified candidates for the fall, in effect ending
> what school officials called the most crippling teacher shortages
> in decades.

So far, so good. Only as one reads on does it become clear that
the way eight thousand new "qualified" teacher candidates
were identified was simply by lowering the standards for certi-
fication. Qualified candidates now include people just entering
teacher education programs, Teach for America recruits with
no qualifications but special variances from the schools, and
other people whose ability to teach poor children is no greater
than that of the so-called unqualified teachers of the past.
Change the language, build a hospital at the bottom of the hill.
As Arthur Levine, president of Teachers College, Columbia
University, says in the article:

> It's a disingenuous claim. New York has reclassified what it means
> to be a certified teacher, and what it means is we will still have
> large numbers of students this fall whose teachers are unprepared
> to teach them.[4]

There are strong similarities between the wise men of
Chelm's suggestions and many of the current generation of
school reform proposals. Reforms under consideration range
from proclaiming unattainable national and state education

goals to mandating that the United States become number one in education throughout the world without having the slightest idea of what "number one" means or how to achieve this fantasy. Other proposals advocate adopting tough teacher evaluations and offering merit pay to teachers without providing support for teacher improvement or having a vision of what good teaching might look like. Voucher and charter school programs are pushed as solutions to educational problems without considering that they are not immune from the same stupid functioning of the public schools they purport to replace. And perhaps worse is the professionalization of stigmatizing students who are not well served by reforms and designating them as "learning disabled" and "attention-deficit disordered" rather than looking to the institutional causes of their indifference, defiance, and failure. Teachers become designated as "special ed," "hyperactive," and "attention-deficit disordered," as if they have the same bogus disorders as their students. Stupidity becomes institutionalized, and having an MA and credentials in a stupid field means that one's entire livelihood is dependent upon maintaining the stupidity system.

The most common theme repeated in the media by politicians and academics who claim a place in the education-reform movement is that current schooling has or will have a negative influence on our nation's economic competitiveness and standing as a world power. Obsession with national power distorts people's perceptions of the problems youngsters face in schools, and most reform proposals end up by leaving out concern for the quality of children's lives.

The question for many of us educators who live in our own versions of Chelm is what to do to escape this infuriating stupidity. Thinking about the pain of living under regimes of stupidity and particularly about the wonderful young teachers

I work with who feel they are compelled to be stupid every day of their working lives reminds me of a quote from Franz Kafka's *The Castle*:

> Dealing directly with the authorities wasn't all that difficult, for no matter how well organized they were, they only had to defend distant and invisible causes on behalf of remote and invisible gentlemen, whereas he, K., was fighting for something vitally close, for himself, and what's more of his own free will . . . [5]

Though we are all familiar with stupidity in our lives, fortunately a certain number of people are always thinking of ways to subvert, oppose, and even eliminate it. Roger, my student, told me a funny story about his reaction to being forced to teach to the scripted program that he knew would undo the work he had already done. He managed to steal some classroom time to keep one of his favorite projects alive. It consisted of telling folktales and fairy tales and then having his students rewrite them as modern stories with contemporary characters and endings. One of the stories he liked to use was "The Emperor's New Clothes." He said the story began to obsess him at faculty meetings and staff training sessions with the "Open Court police." The staff was forced to listen and to comply. They had no input. For him, it was the potential undoing of his own success with his class, and he began to ask the trainers what were to him obvious questions. He wanted to know whether there were statistics to support the new program, or if there was any respect for the children's culture in it. He also asked whether students who failed to go through the program as predicted had other options for learning. The trainers and administrators had no answers, and he told me they were as naked as the emperor, but they had the power. They were not interested in the educational issues or in his particular classroom or work. They wanted alignment above all, no exceptions tolerated. But he knew they had no clothes, and the thought of them as the real fools kept him going for the rest of the academic year. However, the emperor still reigns, so Roger decided he would have to take a year off and reconsider how to continue to serve his students outside of a failure system.

One question that interests me is what became of the child who revealed that the emperor was naked. Did she or he get rewarded and become a national hero? Did his or her action become forgotten as the empire continued to act in naked and brutal ways, and the hustlers and advisers profited from the stupidity system? Did the child give up, internalize the norms of stupidity, and sustain blows to his or her sense of self-worth?

If the child was strong and maintained an open and honest way of confronting stupidity, a rebel might be born. Confronting stupidity when it is sanctioned and so easy to slip into can make for a frustrating life on the margins of self-confidence, employment, and society. It can also lead to major and positive transformations in society, culture, and personal life.

When I was studying philosophy at Harvard in the late 1950s, I remember being intrigued by professors who had fallen under the spell of Ludwig Wittgenstein when they encountered him at Cambridge University. They agonized over traditional philosophical questions, put their hands over their heads, and said, in imitation of their mentor, "God, I am stupid today."

According to many recent accounts, "God, I am stupid today," accompanied by grimaces and expressions of pain, angst, and rage, were characteristics of Wittgenstein's process of addressing with severe honesty and specificity what ap-

peared on the surface to be complex and meaningful philosophical questions. He was a ruthless enemy of stupidity and
confusion—and he considered himself to be one of those vic-
timized by stupidity. For me, that was a profound insight into
how we are all taken in and end up acting against our better
judgment and conscience.

Wittgenstein was seeking to clear away stupidity and
sham, to get people to be clear and explicit about what they
mean by what they say and do, no matter what pain or questioning it might cause. I think he might have agreed with Oscar
Wilde's comment "There is no sin except stupidity." [6]

Wittgenstein's battle with stupidity and pursuit of insane
clarity reminds me of what Jules Henry says at the beginning of
his essay "Sham":

> We all live everyday by sham, anyone who fights against it, makes
> life unbearable. [7]

What was so painful to Rosa, Roger, and Reginald, and to
many other teachers and students I talk to, is that by allowing
themselves to conform to stupid demands, they become experts at sham. In a recent teacher education class I taught on
theater, the students improvised a faculty meeting during
which they were being instructed on how to follow a scripted
lesson while their students were acting up. The teachers all understood the absurdity of the situation and presented what
could be a taxonomy of sham responses that allowed them to
conform while at the same time acknowledge the stupidity of
the situation and maintain some semblance of dignity.

As Henry concludes:

> . . . sanity is nothing more than the capacity to deal with false-
> ness in a false world; and it can take three forms—to believe sham

to be the truth; to see through sham while using it; or to see through sham but fight it . . . we are now in the stage of believing sham to be the truth, while entering the stage of seeing through sham while using it. The third stage is understanding sham and knowing how to fight it. The fourth stage is a world without sham.[8]

I am interested in the third and fourth stages with respect to stupidity: understanding it, knowing how to fight it, and moving toward a world without it. That is where the definition of stupid as "stupefied" comes in. In one of its original meanings, to be stupefied does not mean to be made stupid so much as it means to be astonished, in awe, awakened. It is to experience what the educator and philosopher Maxine Greene has called "wide-awakeness." She describes this state of consciousness as

. . . the recovery of imagination that lessens the social paralysis we see around us and restores the sense that some thing can be done in the name of what is decent and humane. I am reaching toward an idea of imagination that brings an ethical concern to the fore, a concern that, again, has to do with the community that ought to be in the making and the values that give it color and significance. My attention turns back to the importance of wide-awakeness, of awareness of what it is to be in the world. I am moved to recall the existential experience shared by so many and the associated longing to overcome somnolence and apathy in order to choose, to reach beyond.[9]

One of the most powerful examples I know of moving from the state of stupidity to the state of stupefaction and to the social action implied by wide-awakeness comes from the work of Helen Lewis, a former director of the Highlander Center in

New Market, Tennessee, and an adult educator. Helen works in poor Appalachian communities where most of the people are called "hillbillies." The word "hillbilly," according to *Longman's Dictionary of the English Language*, refers to people who come from "culturally unsophisticated" areas, especially the mountains, hills, and valleys of Appalachia. As anyone who has ever seen *Hee-Haw* or *The Beverly Hillbillies* knows, hillbillies are portrayed as ignorant, clumsy, silly, dense—stupid in every way, and an easy butt of jokes and subject to ridicule.

Many of the people Helen works with are sophisticated and fluent in Appalachian culture, which goes back to pre–American Revolutionary times and originates in Scotland, Ireland, and England while having elements of Native American and African American culture as well. Though the people are materially poor, they are not culturally poor, and the general stereotype of hillbilly culture that equates poverty with ignorance is constructed to allow people in the mountains to be exploited by coal companies, land developers, and corporations that profit from mining and exploiting other local resources while dumping toxic waste and creating land erosion. The premise is that stupid people deserve what they get.

One of Helen's goals, as an educator, is to help the people she works with understand how they are exploited and encourage them to organize and create strategies for community development. A major factor that prevents people from taking power over their own lives is accepting images of themselves that celebrate their stupidity and passivity. The hillbilly image is not merely funny to the rest of America but is paralytic if the people being mocked laugh at their own stupidity. And yet people in the mountains often felt that *The Beverly Hillbillies* and *Hee-Haw* were funny.

Helen's educational strategy was to show videos of these TV programs to people in the mountains who were trying to organize themselves and rebuild economically and socially devastated communities. The first time she showed them to a group, people laughed at the stupidity they portrayed. Showing the same program a second time got people quiet and thoughtful—it didn't seem so funny as they began to see themselves as they were displayed to others. The third time, they moved from laughing at hillbilly stupidity to being stupefied, awakened, to the fact that they had been laughing at themselves. As they discussed this progression they became more wide-awake and began to analyze ways in which they were collaborating with the corporate and political interests that exploited them by accepting the premise that they were stupid and worthy of ridicule. The final stage is to become part of an organized effort to counter exploitation.

Stupefaction and wide-awakeness are steps on the road to undoing passivity and stupidity and moving people toward organizing and resisting the stupid demands made upon them. However, it is important to place educational stupidity in the larger context of the apparent need for teachers to act stupidly and for them to become complicit in making their students stupid. One of the central ideas Jules Henry expressed in his *New York Review of Books* article was that "The world is presented to children and adolescents in such a way as to prevent them from getting from school the information necessary to enable them to form an intelligent opinion about the world." [10] I believe this can be extrapolated and paraphrased: "The field of education is presented to prospective and practicing teachers in such a way as to prevent them from getting the information necessary to enable them to form intelligent opinions about learning, teaching, and educational systems."

One way to overcome this situation is for teachers and other educators to be explicit about their stupefaction and to organize around the wide-awakeness that comes from open reflection on their work. This means confronting the painful fact that the media, educational "authorities," and politicians portray teachers as stupid and incapable of making responsible and informed decisions about educational policies and practices. The teaching profession is not innocent here—often, teachers' organizations are willing to accept stupidity as the price of salary and benefit increases.

The right not to be stupid is a human right, and the cost of remaining stupid and submitting to institutional stupidity is a loss of respect for teaching as a moral vocation centered on respect, dignity, and integrity. One pays for aware and conscious stupidity in tears, as it is hard to live with the sense of betrayal that comes from doing stupid things that are not conducive to learning when children's lives are at stake. And in the end it is the children who suffer from the stupidity of the adults. Complicity with stupid systems is an attack upon the young, and the need for educators at all levels to organize and speak out in the service of wide-awake intelligence is urgent these days, even if it means taking personal risks in economically perilous times. We cannot afford to be cowards. Democracy and decency cannot survive compliant stupidity.

2.
Worrying:
Notes Toward a Moral Education
Curriculum Post–9/11

A fair world, a radiant world—but, oh, for whom?[11]
—Yiddish proverb

In 1900, the mathematician David Hilbert gave a speech to
the Second International Congress of Mathematicians meeting
in Paris. The address reflected on the state of mathematics at
the turn of the century and posed twenty-three unanswered
questions that Hilbert thought would determine the shape of
mathematical thinking during the twentieth century. Now, just
a few years into the twenty-first century, we are faced with over-
whelming moral, economic, and social problems that have
been compounded by the traumatic shock of 9/11. What used
to be certain is unclear. Questions about how to portray the
U.S.'s role in the world, about victimization and aggression,
and about good and evil, are played out at every level of society.
It is important at this critical moral juncture for educators to
follow Hilbert's example and try to define what's still unknown
in the field. By posing key questions about our current knowl-

edge of the moral development of children and the effect of education on the development of values, we adults can attempt to help young people navigate the moral minefields of the beginning of the twenty-first century, when we ourselves are at sea.

Sometimes this moral confusion manifests itself in very simple and immediate ways. One of my students who is teaching a second-grade class on a provisional teaching credential encountered three of her students, previously best friends, engaged in a nasty fight about a month after September 11. Two of the three seven-year-old boys were mocking, ridiculing, and punching the third boy, who was crying and screaming, "Why don't you like me anymore? What did I do?"

The teacher, Janice, intervened and sat the three boys down for the usual conflict-resolution session, but, she told me, she knew it wasn't the same old thing that would end up with handshakes and smiles. The boy who was rejected from what was, the day before, his inner circle of friends was Reza, an Iranian American. One of the other boys, Roger, was Jewish, and the third, Jeff, was African American. Roger and Jeff—the "real Americans," as they called themselves—had somehow picked up the notion that their former friend, who was born in California and was not of Arab descent, was an Arab, an enemy, a terrorist, an alien, not a real American. He had to be expelled from their little community and punished for—for what? That was the question that had made the conflict-resolution session so confounding and new.

Previous situations Janice had had to deal with had involved a specific provoking event: someone stole something, or pushed someone; or one child was isolated or another bullied. There were times when these problems had manifested themselves as racism or sexism, but resolution had focused on the immediate provoking event; the problems lurking in the background could be dealt with indirectly. The events were difficult to work through, but were part of the normal process of creating a community consisting of a complex and diverse group of children. The more intractable issues of prejudice and tolerance were addressed throughout Janice's entire curriculum.

However, this particular event, following 9/11, was more difficult for Janice to deal with. The provoking event was not personal. There wasn't any indication of conflict among the three boys and, from Janice's telling of it, the children were very confused about what they were doing. It was a panic response. Roger and Jeff expressed fears about being blown up and bombed and crashed. They expressed fear of Reza's family. He wasn't under the same danger, they insisted; he wouldn't be attacked.

The children were too young to understand the complex problems of the Middle East, or even to know that Reza's father was in exile in the United States for supporting democracy in his homeland. Janice herself felt at a loss to fill in enough information to help the children through this crisis. She was accustomed to dealing with her students' values, but in this case she didn't know where she stood, as she had never thought much about world affairs before 9/11. Her own values were shaken by the event, and she felt uncertain about whom to trust and whom to suspect. She gave up trying to resolve the conflict, and eased the Iranian boy into another group of students who accepted him as a classmate and did not harass him.

Janice did not resolve the moral issues and was lost herself. Her values were threatened by 9/11, and she was as morally unsettled as her students. She also had to face, without preparation, the phenomenon of a sudden shift in values on the part of her students. Children who had cared about one another, played together, and hung out one day had become enemies overnight without any one of them doing anything differently. Their behavior and attitudes, and the values they embodied, had changed. The issues were not personal but manifested themselves in very personal ways. And what about their values? Had they changed overnight? If so, what were the specifics of those changes? How developed were they, and how developed were their teacher's values when she had to deal with their values? This leads to the central question: how much can we say we know with confidence about children's development of moral values?

Hilbert, in his 1900 speech, made some remarks about the importance of problem posing to the health of a discipline. It is useful to keep this idea in mind when reflecting on developing a program to understand children's moral development in a time of intense moral anxiety:

> Who of us would not be glad to lift the veil behind which the future lies hidden; to cast a glance at the next advances of our science and at the secrets of its development during future centuries. What particular goals will there be towards which the leading mathematical spirits of coming generations will strive? What new methods and new facts will new centuries disclose in the wide and rich field of mathematical thought? . . . we must let the unsettled questions pass before our minds . . .
>
> It is difficult and often impossible to judge the value of a problem correctly in advance; for the final award depends upon the gain which science obtains from the problem. Nevertheless, we can ask whether there are general criteria which mark a good mathematical problem. An old French mathematician said, "A mathematical theory is not to be considered complete until you have made it so clear that you can explain it to the first man whom you meet on the street." [12]

It is much easier to specify unsolved problems in the realm of mathematics than in the realm of moral development. The line between proof and conjecture, which is agreed upon by most mathematicians, is not clear when values are at issue. In even the most sophisticated study of children there is always the danger of generalizing from a small sample of children to all of humanity. The roles that culture, history, class, gender, race, and religion play in development provide additional complexities for the study and teaching of moral values. This is particularly true in a world where communication is almost instant and where conflicting value systems contend for young people's attention in school, the family, the media, and on the streets. The teacher of morality is also a moral person acting on the basis of personally held values that may not be consistent with the way in which students' parents or others in authority believe moral development should take place.

Children also receive mixed moral messages from the adults around them. Recently one of my teacher-credential students came into my office crying about a serious fight in her class that day. She had been trained in conflict resolution and for several months had worked with her students on nonviolent solutions. Yet that day when she took aside the children who were fighting, one of them told her that he was just doing what his parents had told him to do: defending himself. She called the parents, and they confirmed what the boy said. They wanted their son to learn how to fight back and didn't want him to back down when challenged. The teacher's message was overridden by the parents' values.

Yet if everyone in the class always fought back when challenged, things would end in chaos. I was as frustrated as she was, and we responded by developing a curriculum on nonviolent self-defense. We didn't want to sanction fighting, but accepted the premise that self-defense was a necessary survival skill on the streets and sometimes in the classroom. We're still working on the problem.

Over the almost forty years I have been working with children and reflecting on their lives, I have faced a number of questions about children's moral growth that I cannot answer and that I don't believe any current theory can answer, either. Recently, the events of September 11 have indelibly shaped attitudes toward violence, conflict, threat, and aggression—changes that show up in the schools as well. I want to share these questions in the spirit of Hilbert, and suggest that speculating on them may lead to a richer understanding of the way children think about the uncertainties and problems of the adult world and become moral actors themselves. I also hope that raising the questions will lead educators in these uncertain times to pay particular attention to moral struggles and to ground their own work in explicit, compassionate moral values.

I don't believe in moral neutrality, yet I also feel uncomfortable imposing my own values, centered around social and economic justice, on children no matter how gently I do it. I feel equally uncomfortable, however, with the idea that young people should be abandoned in their search for a moral world. I have never been convinced that moral development will take place naturally: culture and the social world are too powerful mediators of growth even to conceive of pure moral growth unfettered by mediated experiences.

Therefore, in the spirit of David Hilbert, I want to pose ten groups of questions about children's values and development that have not been adequately answered and are often overlooked.

Question 1: Altruism/Competition

Are children evil, and do they need to be corrected and guided—or are they pure spirits who, left unfettered by the constraints of culture and adult control, will be naturally kind and pure? Are they competitive and driven by the need to excel and show their superiority? Or do they have to be shaped and driven and seduced into conformity to adult norms?

What is the nature of the child? This question is at the center of debates on how education should be controlled or conducted, and reflects moral debates within the adult world that may be insolvable. Are young suicide bombers born that way, or made by social circumstances? Are suburban youngsters who kill born to kill, or driven to rage and unreason? What is the role of kindness under conditions of oppression? All of these questions lead to the need to study moral development in the social, economic, and political contexts of the world, not merely in the few children who become the subject of academic studies of moral development.

One particular aspect of this question has been underexplored: what is the role of altruism in children's moral development? Altruism is, according to the philosopher Thomas Nagel, "a willingness to act in consideration of the interests of other people without the need of ulterior motives."[13]

A burning love for poor and oppressed people and a developing sense of the necessity of justice—and not solely some abstract conception of moral principle—are often the guiding forces behind the sacrifices that revolutionaries are willing to make in the name of the future. This love is a force that has led to the transformation of many societies and is what keeps resistance and opposition to authoritarianism alive under the most repressive conditions. The question I want to raise is: *what is the role of love in the growth of morality?* And what is the relationship between the love between mother, father, and child, or community and child, and the more generalized and empathic love for all people that some of us develop? How does that love get conveyed to children so that it becomes a driving force in their lives?

In Stephen J. Gould's column for *Natural History* magazine, he often talked about the role of altruism in evolution and the many studies of the role of altruistic behavior in binding animal communities and contributing to the survival of the whole group. The failure of many developmental theories to recognize altruism as a central force in moral growth is troublesome and leads to the shallowness of their descriptions of young life.

Piagetian developmental learning theory, for example, denies both affect and love a central place in early cognitive growth. It also elevates self-centeredness to a principle of moral development. Self-interest is the driving force of Piagetian theory, and yet there is no more evidence to support that assumption than there is to support the centrality of altruism, empathy, and other forms of disinterested love. I believe that we are far from understanding the forces at work in infants' and children's worlds, and that much more careful observation over a wider range of cultural, economic, and social conditions has to be done before conclusions are drawn. In addition, we have to be careful about the filters we use when we speak about and observe behaviors we don't directly understand.

This means repudiating much of current thinking about children and reexamining the observations that led to accepted ideas and assumptions about child development. However, in a world where social and economic conditions are fluid, and novel forms of organizing the conditions of life are likely to emerge, it makes sense to pose new questions, make fresh observations, and reconsider old theories in light of the social, historical, and economic conditions that gave rise to them.

For example, what is the moral relationship between violence and nonviolence when they are both motivated by altruistic love? Are Nelson Mandela or Malcolm X at a lower stage of moral development than Mahatma Gandhi and Martin Luther King Jr., as Lawrence Kohlberg's stages of moral development assume? More generally, is nonviolence a higher form of moral action than revolutionary violence? In the case of child development, are the children throwing stones in Palestine less moral than those in other places who face oppression stoically and passively? This even leads to the question of whether being nonviolent can't in certain circumstances be a manifestation of loss of hope or of paralyzing fear rather than of moral superiority.

The question of the moral role of violence and nonviolence in resisting oppression may seem rather remote from the moral development of bourgeois children growing up in Western Europe and the United States. However, the need to take a moral stand with respect to resistance against or compliance with oppression faces children and their families throughout the world. We have to be worried in the current climate of fear and eternal war against unknown terrorists about whether our children are being educated to abandon their altruistic instincts and embrace the idea that violence and war are a normal part of everyday life.

Question 2: Choice

How can one study the role of choice in moral development? If there is a tension between "good and evil," between altruism and greed, then how does a child decide how to position herself or himself on the moral spectrum? I have seen families in which some children are angry and violent and are perfectly willing to hurt other people to get what they want. Other children in the same family are incapable of violence, are loving toward others, and are determined to resolve conflicts and eliminate violence. This is not a romantic assessment of these compassionate youngsters, as sometimes they do not survive precisely because of their peacemaking.

My knowledge of the burden of being forced to make moral choices at an early age was expanded recently during conversations with a number of Southeast Asian teenagers and young adults who were caught up in war and revolution from the time of their births. These youngsters speak of how painful it is to have to hurt other people in order to protect oneself; they have stories to tell about moral and immoral action amid decisions made when they were as young as five and six that might, if taken seriously, lead to major reconceptualizations of how children develop morally. Some had to kill in order to free themselves; others had to steal food in order to make it to the refugee camp. And others saw their parents brutalized and murdered before they were able to escape. And yet they are now compassionate, loving people. What did they choose? How did they develop? Their experiences make the usual middle-class studies of the moral development of children in the United States seem tiny and all too arrogant.

Another way to rephrase these questions is: *what existential situations force children to make decisions and articulate values, and how do these situations effect moral growth and development?* Existential situations are situations in which it is impossible not to make a choice. They provide dilemmas that force a person to define who he or she is, what is worth fighting and taking risks for, and what values are worth acting upon. For example, what happens when a five-year-old has to choose between his or her mother or father when a marriage breaks up? This dilemma forces an existential choice upon a child, as do the following situations:

* *deciding whether to forgive someone who has hurt you very badly*

* *being forced to decide whether to physically prevent some-one from hurting himself or to let him go ahead and do it*

* *deciding whether to intervene when you witness someone hurting another person*

* *hurting someone who is vulnerable in order to gain atten-tion or power, or forgoing that opportunity based on com-passion or principle*

Existential situations imply will, and raise the question of choice and self-determination in a child's life. What is the role of will in development? What is the nature of moral choice and the construction of a moral world? What are the constraints on such choice? Any theory of moral growth has to account for freedom and establish whether set patterns of development or dearly held values can be overridden by choice. Is there yet a language in education adequate to speak to these dilemmas? It is not enough to assert, dogmatically, as some theories do, that there is an invariable sequence of stages of moral development or to deny the existence of choice in human consciousness when situations arise that force moral choice and result in un-expected moral transformations.

Question 3: Contradictions

What is the role of contradiction and dialectical development in the moral life of the child? A contradiction is a situation in which two opposite and apparently irreconcilable conditions present themselves simultaneously to a person as a problem. For example, a poor child in the United States who watches TV knows that she or he lives in a rich country. Being poor in a rich country, especially one that claims that anyone can be-come successful, is a contradiction and a problem to a child.

49

The opposites, poverty and wealth, are presented in an irreconcilable form for the child who cannot change her or his situation of life. Though authorities and scholars may deny it, very young children have sophisticated and painful analyses of their place in the world. And these contradictions may well be the generating forces of rage that sometimes explodes into violence.

Racism also presents a contradiction to the child who is discriminated against and at the same time is told that she or he lives in a free country where everyone has the same rights. It presents a reality problem. It is possible to live with the contradiction and even to be driven crazy by it, or to plan to become defiant and resolve the contradiction through some form of action. How do young children think about such problems? Clearly they are not passive, yet all too infrequently do they have an opportunity to discuss the contradictions facing them. Perhaps this is because adults don't have the answers and therefore avoid the questions.

At what point in life does the decision to reject the status quo develop? How do children conceptualize their own powers to transform the world? What is the role of daydreaming, active fantasy, and role-playing in developing plans and forming a self-image? What new forms of living arise from facing and overcoming contradictions—from participating in dialectical struggles? And, finally, what are the distinctions between growth that takes place dialectically and growth that takes place in an orderly and stage-determined way? Does development encompass both forms of growth—and, if so, how? All of these questions are currently open, and any adequate account of moral growth must consider them.

Question 4: Death and Madness

How does a child's experience with death affect his or her perception of right and wrong? Think of children growing up in a country experiencing famine, or of children in Latin America suffering the horrors of the death squads; of children growing up on urban streets in the United States for whom dodging bullets and stepping over dead bodies is an everyday experience. Think of children whose relatives are going to fight other people's wars like those in Iraq and Colombia. And think of middle-class children for whom death is often hidden. What are the effects of the hiding of death upon moral action, and what are the effects of the presence of death upon it? When do youngsters become hardened and cruel, and when do they become compassionate and gentle, in the face of death? How does this vary from child to child and culture to culture? Is there an undervaluing of life for children who have experienced too much early death or is that effect more common with children who have been hidden from dying?

I will never forget a scene I witnessed from my classroom in Harlem in 1962. A junkie had died overnight, and his body was lying in the hallway of a tenement building across the street from the school. After calling the police I watched five- and six-year-olds as well as some of my students walk over the body to get across the street to school. I asked my sixth-grade students about it, and they said I was naive, that it happened all the time, and besides, they didn't want to stay at home waiting for the police to come and rough people up in their investigation. I asked them if the same thing could happen to them and was greeted by such a glacial silence that I went on with my lesson plan and didn't get back to the issue of early death and survival until the next week.

It is particularly important for many teachers to understand the relationship between early experiences of death and the development of values. Just a few months ago two young men were gunned down near a school I work with. The children at the school knew them, and this wasn't the first time they had experienced young people dying violently. A few months later a young girl was burned to death in a fire at her apartment. Do children respond in the same way to a fire death as they do to a gun death? How do they think about the difference? Does gun violence make some students hard and others timid and anxious? How does religion shape these experiences? And what is a teacher to do, especially if he or she believes in justice and has a commitment to the idea that there is some inner goodness in every child?

I agonize over these questions, as do many teachers I know who refuse to give up on any child. But I also find myself tempted to give up on some youngsters who act and talk and live in ways that are beyond my reach and in some cases are quite simply frightening. What I think is needed is an attempt to share how teachers deal with young death, and to talk with young people about their perceptions and then follow up on the conversations years later. Do values evolve? Are there some early experiences that simply inhibit growth or twist it? We need to take a close look at this and elaborate on some of the interesting work currently being done on youth and resiliency. What experiences and strengths shape the values of resilient youth? What is the role of TV? Does the endless war on invisible terrorists mold the children's values? How does moral development fare during times of war, social hysteria, or actual murderous assault such as what happened on 9/11 and in the U.S. assaults on the governments of Chile, Panama, and Nicaragua? And how does privilege mold values? What sensitivity leads some children to adopt values that accept the exploitation of their peers or to become racist or homophobic and others to be compassionate, bold, and willing to take risks for other people? These questions need to be explored if we are to develop profound insights into the nature of growth and development, and are much more crucial, from my point of view, than the questions of brain function and cognitive development, which, in an attempt to be "scientific," avoid the moral commitment every researcher and teacher needs to acknowledge.

Question 5: Hope

The fifth question occurred to me after an experience I had with a seven-year-old girl named Lori who was in my class several years ago. Lori lived with her mother, who had serious personal problems. When tension at home became almost unbearable Lori tried to run away from home and school. Often at the end of the morning in school, before the bus came, she would come up to me and say she was just going to walk home and leave school. Naturally I had to follow her and bring her back. Most of the times, she returned when I called, but sometimes I had to pick her up and carry her, screaming and struggling to get free, back into the building. Once back, I tried gently to coax her into thinking through ways of solving her problems without getting hurt or lost in the woods.

On one of those days, Lori said, "Okay, I'm going to do something," and sat down and drew a picture of a yellow cab and told me she was going to steal one. I asked, "What's this all about?" And in a very serious, adult voice, she said, "My mom has a drug problem, and is always fighting with the men she brings home. My life is very complicated, so I'm going to take my cab and drive away. When I find a nice place, I'll give the taxi back and find some friends. I'm going to make a new life."

That statement was a powerful affirmation of faith in the

possibility of goodness and the power of the moral imagination. Lori did believe that she could think out moral values and restructure the moral world. That experience led to this unanswered question about the moral growth of children: what is the relationship between hope and morality? And as the phenomenon of suicide bombing has dramatized, what is the relationship between hopelessness and the sanctity of life? How is moral development shaped by the way in which the world surrounding a child fits on what could be called the hope/hopelessness continuum?

Recently I discovered the three volumes of *The Principle of Hope,* by Ernst Bloch, an East German who settled in West Germany after the building of the Berlin Wall.[14] It is a complex analysis of hope as a feature of moral and political life. Bloch, who died in 1977, was one of the major theoreticians of humanistic socialism. His book is an affirmation of the need for daydreaming and utopian thinking in order to keep the possibility of decency alive, if only in the imagination. In the book he claims that accepting the inevitability of competition and poverty implied in capitalist ideology leads to the denial of the power of utopian daydreams and is a cause of hopelessness. On a child's level this would be the same as believing that it is impossible to make things better, that romantic visions of possible worlds should be abandoned and that one should simply accept as fact the thought that poverty can never be eliminated, that some people are superior to others, and that it is foolish to even imagine that everyone can be happy. It also represents trying to enforce on children the simplistic notions of "us" and "them," good and evil, and in particular the notion that "we" are absolutely good and "they" are absolutely evil. Since this vision is being projected from the top of our society, it is particularly important to think of ways to nurture the complex, hopeful imaginations of the young and not subject them to a morality that denies thoughtful understanding and the capacity to question authority. Of course, these last show how my own moral values have emerged. But to speak about morality and to study and question it is as much a moral act as a research challenge.

Bloch's work gives rise to some interesting elaborations on the question about the relationship of hope and morality. What is the morality of capitalism, and how does it play out in the lives of children in our society? Are moral values learned in the same way by all of the children in the society, or does learning differ from class to class, individual to individual, culture to culture, etc.? How does utopian thinking develop, and what is the relationship of utopian thought, daydreaming, and the active imagination? What would communication of values across cultures look like? And are there ultimate irreconcilable differences within the moral world that imply that morality will always be a contested field that will often be contested in the lives of children who are expected to perpetuate values?

The moral imagination of children needs to be studied through artistic expression, fantasy play, and casual conversation. I've noticed when teaching chess and checkers to five- and six-year-olds that they have no problem modifying rules by inventing new ones and creating rule-governed games to play on the spot. I had a chess club for five- and six-year-olds, and it was marvelous to watch the children experiment with game forms and consciously decide to play out different variations of moves and captures. I've wondered whether children don't also play with the rules of living and judging in a similar way, and have more wide-ranging and flexible moral imaginations than adults. It's possible that children entertain the wickedest as well as the most saintly ways of valuing people and things, and that adult values result from interactions among imagined worlds, joyful and hurtful experiences, and the systems adults try to impose and teach. I don't know the answer to these questions but believe there is fertile ground for speculation and experimentation here.

Another way of looking at the question of the relationship of hope to imagination and morality is to ask, *"What happens to values when hope is eroded?"* What are the moral consequences of the erosion of hope in childhood? How do we speak to children about moral issues? How do we speak about children? How do we deal with the complex interplay between learning compassionate values and learning competitive values that they may need to survive? In particular, what are the circumstances under which hope survives and people acquire the utopian mentality that is necessary to embark on a lifelong struggle for compassion and justice?

I suspect that the secret of the survival of the dream of a free and just life has to do with both the goodness that characterizes some part of the spirit and the secret teachings of hope that even the most oppressed and troubled people manage to pass on to their children despite their suffering. It also has to do with the central role of respect and dignity. For some people in the United States and throughout the world, however, this tradition may be endangered by the cold intensification of the horrors of the twentieth century in this early part of the twenty-first.

Question 6: The Role of Teachers and Other Influences

What is the role of teaching in moral development? The Russian psychologist Lev Vygotsky talks about teaching being maximally effective in what he calls "the zone of proximal development." His meaning is easy to grasp from this example: Suppose a person has mastered word processing on a computer and is trying to extend his or her skills to programming.

The word-processing skills and the familiarity and ease with using a computer provide a good base for beginning to learn programming. The demands of programming are different, however, and involve greater knowledge of how the computer's logic works and how the computer can be instructed to follow certain rules. The learning gap between the knowledge of computers and word processing already mastered, and the programming to be learned, is an example of a zone of proximal development. Within it, the learner has partial mastery, but still faces many learning challenges. According to Vygotsky, it is when a learner is working within this zone of proximal development that teaching is most helpful. In the example above, a few hints about how the computer executes instructions and how feedback and looping work can lead to quick and thorough mastery. Without this help the learner may flounder and get lost or discouraged.

Is it possible to ask when considering the role of teaching in moral development whether there is an equivalent zone of proximal development in moral growth? Are there moments of moral exploration where hints, support, and shared experience nurture development? Complementary to this is the question of whether it is appropriate for a teacher to be explicit about his or her moral values in the classroom. Is didactic teaching effective, or are storytelling and parable making more to the point when one is struggling with moral issues? What is the role of interpersonal learning and shared experience in moral development?

I have tried over the years to figure out how to express my values in a context where my students don't feel coerced into assenting to them. In fact, I've encouraged dissent. I keep on urging my students to disagree with my values, which are progressive, left-wing, and definitely not mainstream. I also tell stories about dissent within my family, about years' long arguments with very close friends. The idea is to encourage thoughtful debate about values and to acquaint students with ideas that are often unfamiliar to them, conscience being the one least discussed in schools.

How students decide what they believe is still a mystery to me, and no matter how much academic literature I've read, I am yet to be convinced that we have the slightest idea how values develop in young people and during the course of their adult lives. One thing that is certainly not adequately studied is how values change, and what kinds of events and experiences provoke those changes. Fiction and poetry often concern those profound questions of development, but educators remain silent about them.

Question 7: Transformations

What kinds of transformations do people undergo in life that mold their moral values? I have heard many people say their values were changed post-9/11. Some doves became reluctant (and morally tormented) hawks, and some very conservative, pro-war people became thoughtful resisters to violence and war. Changes in values don't go one way. How do children change their values or grow into new ways of seeing the world? How do adults respond to crises, think under pressure, reflect upon unanticipated experiences, and reconstellate their value systems? Those of us who have experienced the civil rights and anti–Vietnam War movements have been through personal transformations and have seen others whose moral lives have been reconstructed during struggle. As an educator I have also seen many young children who have had to take moral stands when they and their families were involved in war, protest, violence, and the struggle to survive exile, resettlement, and the often desperate attempt to create a normal and peaceful life.

Working through this, I've been thinking about a taxonomy of the transformation of values, both for young people and for adults, and want to share my latest, incomplete, and tentative efforts in the spirit of this chapter on questioning.

One of the reasons people undergo transformations of values is the result of an act of discovery. Some experiences raise major questions about your ideals, values, prejudices, preferences, and everyday behavior. Sometimes these are as dramatic as the events of 9/11, but they can be very intimate, like discovering something about your parents or hearing a teacher say something racist, or finding some caring adult who gives you strength you didn't know you had. Here are some general categories of discovery that I've experienced in myself, my family, friends, and students:

  i. feeling used, deceived
  ii. reaching limits
  iii. feeling or discovering that one has been miseducated
  iv. experiencing the opportunity to speak out when you've previously been silenced
  v. learning that your privileges have been hurting others
  vi. discovering others' lives and their pain and suffering
  vii. realizing that, however hard your life is, there are people who have stood in opposition to similar oppression and exploitation
  viii. having serendipitous encounters that force you to confront new realities
  ix. uncovering new skills and capacities in yourself

This is not an exhaustive list, but there are challenges here. What counts for a moral discovery? Who prepares young people to encounter moral dilemmas and articulate their values? How does goodness survive in the midst of chaos, disorder, violence, and deception? As an act of free association, here are other categories of transformation. Each category requires an essay of its own showing how complex moral life and its transformations are, especially in times of trouble:

i. not caring to be safe anymore
ii. a forced change
iii. epiphanies, conversions
iv. charismatic leaders
v. education
vi. "new ideas," paradigm changes
vii. existential moments—times when you are forced to make major decisions that require personal changes and questions of moral identity and responsibility
viii. wanting to be good (to make the values you grew up with work in specific and concrete ways rather than betray your church, family, or friends)
ix. committing class suicide
x. symbolic encounters—changes wrought through the arts, encounters with images, stories, narratives of some sort that move you on a profound level and lead to life changes
xi. learning new information that was previously concealed or distorted
xii. touches with death and dying—with mortality

Though these categories overlap with others mentioned in this chapter, the context of transformation matters. How do people change, or why don't they change? Why do people assent to wars they don't believe in or sacrifice their children because of abject poverty? How do children develop values concerning not just themselves but war and violence both within and beyond the family? And finally, what is the etiology of their conceptions of goodness? Do Palestinian children, for example, transform their values in the same way Israeli children do? Do children in East Los Angeles go through the same transformations as children in Beverly Hills? To me, these are central, unaddressed moral-development questions that are often glossed over by academic studies, which generalize the lives of a small number of carefully chosen American children to draw conclusions about all children.

Question 8: Faith, Religion, and Other Forms of Reverential Motivation

More significantly, there is also inadequate consideration of this eighth, related question: What is the role of faith and religious experience in the growth of moral values? How do children develop religious values?

Religious experience and belief play no role in the work of behaviorists and most developmental theorists, and yet for many children in the world, it is central to their moral development. Robert Coles's work is an exception, documenting, among other examples, the importance of religious belief in the experience of the young people who risked their lives to desegregate schools in the South during the civil rights movement. Many Muslim youth refer to their religious beliefs as spurs to their actions of opposition to Israel, and Orthodox Jewish youngsters act on their beliefs as well. Specific phenomenological studies of the religious experiences of children and the relationship of these experiences to moral action are, however, likely to be very informative about the complex relations between conveying values and having those values accepted and internalized. Religion is often one motivating factor that moves children to participate in social action and to develop conceptions about the "other" that determine the parameters of their

61

personal, social, and political lives among their peers and as adults.

Question 9: Silences, Lies, Indirection, and Evasion

Other essential moral questions worth study post–9/11 deal with issues of authenticity. What is the moral effect of the unspoken, the silences, of all the events and feelings surrounding one that are never explicitly acknowledged? What is the role of skeletons in the closet? Of whiskey bottles hidden in a bookshelf? Of unwanted children and parents who hate each other? Of racial fear, and greed, intolerance, and unrequited love?

Answering these questions would involve a study of the role of sham in our lives, and of vulnerability. It would consider people afraid to speak out, individual as well as social censorship of ideas and the suffocating of feelings. This study could provide the possibility of understanding the unformed nature of many children's moral values and the confusion they face in committing themselves to values in an uncertain and compromised world.

The role of sham and the unspoken in children's lives leads to a methodological question: *When can one rely upon the answers a child gives to a charged moral question?* What are the grounds for believing a response to a question or poll involving values? This is particularly important when dealing with oppressed and minority peoples for whom not speaking the truth can be a conscious strategy of survival, a technique for protecting people one cares about, or concealing one's culture and values from those regarded as enemies. Myles Horton once told me an Appalachian Mountains story that illustrates how fully children can understand and become part of a system of deliberate misrepresentation. It seems there was a girl, about eight or nine, who was confronted by a visiting social worker.

The social worker asked the girl where her father was, and the girl replied, "I don't know." To which the social worker responded, "Well, does he work? What does he do for a living?"

The girl replied in the same way to all of these questions: "I don't know." So the social worker went back to his office and wrote up a report saying that the girl must be slightly retarded and the family must have a lot of problems. Of course the girl knew that her father was out in the woods making bootleg liquor, and had learned that when a stranger asks a question, especially a stranger who looks like a social worker or a revenue agent, you lie to them. Lying was culturally sanctioned: if you don't lie, you'll get in more trouble than if you do, because telling the truth might interfere with the family income and get someone arrested.

Lying is not just the province of oppressed people. During the 1989 governorship race in the state of Virginia, the exit polls predicted that Douglass Wilder, the Democratic Party candidate, who is African American, was well ahead. However, when the votes were counted, the poll turned out to be wrong. The race was neck and neck, one of the closest in the history of the state. The only way to account for the failure of the polls, according to many reports in the media, was the likelihood that many of the white Democrats who were polled had lied and said they'd voted for Wilder though they actually had voted for the white Republican candidate. The *Times* went on to say that it would have been embarrassing socially for many of these white Democrats to admit that they'd voted along race lines, so they just lied—no big deal.

Anybody involved in moral development in society has to consider culturally sanctioned or personally motivated lying as they ask questions dealing with sensitive moral issues. Lying and truth-telling are important linguistic issues with serious social consequences. People (children included) guess at the questioners' values and give what they believe is the sanctioned view in order to look good, deceive, or avoid trouble. Asking sensitive questions as a means of discovering a person's moral values is a delicate matter, and any conclusions based exclusively on that method must be looked upon with reservations. One implication of this is that teachers have to learn about their students, the community in which they work, and the sensitive issues that affect the community's language if they are to understand what the children are saying.

The same issues obtain where there is inequality in the social structure: what is the effect of conventional moral values on an oppressed group within a society? Oppressed people do not live by the same conventions as their oppressors, since conventional morality sanctions oppression. If, for example, conventional morality claims that poverty is an evil that can be avoided by hard work and that therefore poor people are evil, the poor can accept these ideas only at the cost of their self-respect and hope.

Conventional morality usually reflects the ideology of the ruling class, and one must always ask: What is the relationship between conventional morality and the morality of liberation?

For some people and their children, development entails consciously rejecting conventional morality or skipping by it altogether, and moving to another level of value that justifies resistance and revolt. For others, it consists of socially sanctioned playing dumb in order to get the dominant culture off your back.

In that context, one cannot speak intelligently about the moral development of children without taking into account the ten-year-olds in Soweto who refused to speak Afrikaans and set off the school boycotts in South Africa; the child soldiers throughout the world, the street children in Brazil; the equally young children who are involved in the intifada; and, closer to home, the eight-, nine-, and ten-year-olds in Birmingham, Alabama, during the civil rights movement who, before Dr. Martin Luther King Jr. supported children demonstrating against segregation, went out without their parents' permission and forced King to support them.

I think that the possibilities of moral growth between the ages of five and twelve are much more complex than academic theoreticians have ever conceptualized, and it is incumbent upon us to learn from the children who are engaged in struggle or are the victims of adult struggles. As students of childhood, we must be humble rather than dogmatic, learn how to win the trust of children rather than suppose that our protocols and methods will trick them into telling the truth about their values. In order to do this, however, we will probably be called upon to take a stand in their moral struggles. Learning the truth requires no less a commitment on our parts.

Question 10: Research and Generalization

What is a justified generalization from a sample, and how many ways does a sample have to be qualified when a researcher applies its conclusions to people who were not in the sample? Many "conclusions" made about the moral development of all children in the world are actually based on a few children in the United States or Western Europe. In particular I am concerned about any claims that small clinical studies of moral development (some, for example, made in expensive private schools) make about *all* children. Piagetians, in particular, talk as if the conclusions based on samples of fewer than ten children are universal. Indeed, that habit is found throughout the literature of educational psychology. Tests and programs are then based on these studies, and children are subjected to classification and stigmatization by people who administer these tests and impose programs on children and teachers alike, all for a not inconsiderable profit.

What size sample would be necessary to establish a universally applicable statement about all children? Of course that would have to depend upon the nature of the characteristics studied. Universal conclusions are particularly difficult to draw when it comes to the growth of moral values, given the impact of culture, religion, gender, class, and geography on defining a life. Is a sample of one hundred or one thousand or ten thousand adequate to say that something applies to a billion children? I don't know, but researchers must be explicit in justifying the criteria they use for selecting a sample and drawing conclusions about applying their results to a population beyond that sample. That may mean using a cumbersome, adjective-laden language to describe results. Surely it is more honest and less likely to be damaging to say "the thirty-two white, middle-class, seven-year-old, private-school males studied all manifested self-centered values" than to claim that "children of seven have self-centered values." This issue cuts across particular theoretical stances and should be the subject of profession-wide speculation and agreement.

I was particularly irked when, at a meeting several years ago, experts talked about the passive, selfish values of Generation X kids. There was a general tone of smugness and condescension on the part of the people who were surveying the attitudes of that generation—as if it were a uniform group with collective attitudes. My three children, all activists currently engaged in protesting war and unthinking globalization, are unselfish, highly generous, and loving people—and are part of that age group. So are their friends, who do the most interesting things imaginable and have a highly honed social consciousness. I mentioned that, and the main expert said that my examples were a statistically insignificant part of the sample and therefore didn't count for anything. My response was disproportionate to the calm and arrogant professionalism the statistician made. Who counts and who doesn't and who interprets the counting? These are all moral issues that affect the lives of young people.

By Way of Conclusion

I'd like to conclude by returning to David Hilbert, quoted at the beginning of this chapter, who says, "Mathematical science is in my opinion an indivisible whole, an organism whose vitality is conditioned upon the connection of its parts," and claims that the more learned about the answers to the questions he poses, the clearer will be the road to grasping the "organic unity" of the field of mathematics.[15] I want to expand on Hilbert's remarks and suggest that an understanding of the unity of the child, the whole of the person, and the organic nature of the social group are the goals of the study of human growth. The questions posed in this chapter are simply attempts to clear the path a bit, bring out the tentative nature of current knowledge, and raise the unsettling possibility that the best we can do when studying the moral child is to come up with approximations to the living child who is free to make a moral world for herself or himself and in the process confound all our theories.

Part II

The Joy

3.

Write It in the Sky:
Imagining the World Otherwise

(for Maxine Greene)

There was a child went forth every day,
And the first object he looked upon and received with
Wonder or pity or love or dread, that object he became,
And that object became part of him for the day or a
certain part of the day . . . or for many years or
stretching cycles of years.[16]

        —Walt Whitman

ANDREA WAS a pony named Pegasus; Ellen was Jill, the mother horse; and Sasha was their pet dog, Wonder. Wonder went everywhere that Pegasus went, and whenever the pony got into trouble, Wonder would run home to Jill, who always arrived in time to rescue Pegasus. Andrea, Ellen, and Sasha, all age five at the time and in my kindergarten class, played these roles for days and could sustain a single story over the course of several weeks. I watched them work their way through many scenarios, each of which had a crisis, a rescue, and a time of healing. Pegasus would fall in a hole, break a leg while running straight down a mountainside, get bitten by a rattlesnake, or attacked by a mountain lion. In each instance, Wonder would find her way home and bring Jill back to save and heal Pegasus. The roles were all positive: Pegasus was the courageous explorer, Wonder the rescuer, and Jill the healer. The three girls had worked out a way to play without competition, and to act out positive sides of themselves in a situation where they didn't need any other child to be the enemy or aggressor. Their fantasy play had a balance and elegance that I've rarely seen in child's fantasy play, and enabled them to vary the situation with no loss of interest or intensity and continue in those roles for several months.

The endless variations of a single narrative with the structure adventure/trouble/rescue/healing provided a collective way for Andrea, Ellen, and Sasha to explore roles that were not usual in their daily encounters with others. Andrea was a shy, scared child who was always afraid of falling or cutting herself. The adventurer she became in the role of Pegasus was an experiment in stretching out, a rehearsal of a stronger self she had decided to become. Ellen was aggressive and the opposite of the healer that she became in the game. In class she seemed to enjoy instigating mischief and controlling others. In the game she was nurturing, nonaggressive, and gentle, which is now very much part of her adult personality. Sasha at the time was in mourning. Her mother and father had just broken up, and she cried a lot and had the saddest face and limpest body. In class she did things mechanically and without joy, though before the crisis she was always lively and quick with a funny story. As Wonder the rescue dog, she seemed to be able to throw off her present sorrow and become that joyful self again.

It's rare that I've observed children's play that fit so well with the needs and aspirations of the players, and that had so little of the spirit of competition in it. Usually things are messier, especially with boys' play. Dominance often figures in fantasy play, and some children force roles on others. Good and evil characters with unresolvable disagreements emerge, and there is a fragile balance between conflicts that are within the fantasy and those that spill out into the children's everyday realities. None of this happened with Pegasus, Jill, and Wonder.

While the three girls played, they carried on conversations on two different levels. They talked to one another both in character and out of character. For example, Andrea would say to the other girls, "This time I'm going swimming," and then say, in character, "Jill, can I go swimming?" to which Ellen would reply, "Only if you're careful," and Sasha would bark approval. They maintained the fiction while creating a narrative for their actions. They acted with such conviction that their usual selves receded and seemed to have no effect upon the action. In the British theater there is a term called "corpsing." An actor corpses when she or he falls out of character and turns the character they are playing into a dead body. Andrea, Ellen, and Sasha did not corpse. In fact, I have rarely seen children corpse during fantasy play, though I have seen children say, in their narrator's voice, "Let's not play anymore," when they consciously choose to stop playing or leave the game.

I have tried to engage in such sustained fantasy play myself as an adult and have even occasionally convinced friends to join with me in a conscious attempt to reexperience the fullness of childhood imaginings. Only in the context of improvisation or formal theater, with a teacher or audience and a set theme or script, have we been able to approximate the suspension of our own personalities and the complete absorption in fantasy play that young children manifest in imagining the world to be otherwise.

Children not only create and then merge into their own fantasy roles. They accept one another's characters, and spend time in fairly sophisticated conversations about role definition. For example, I remember a conversation between Andrea and Sasha over the powers of Pegasus. Andrea insisted that Pegasus could fly, and Sasha said that she had no trouble with Pegasus flying, except that, if she flew (Pegasus was female, according to Andrea), then Wonder couldn't follow her on adventures. Andrea agreed that it was a problem, and they agreed that when Pegasus had to fly, Wonder could ride on her back. Sasha didn't want Wonder to be a flying dog, but didn't mind Wonder hitching a ride now and then.

Ellen also had a problem: What was she to do when the other two went on an adventure? She didn't want to wait around outside of the game and then just jump into play when a rescue was needed. She wanted to be playing at the same time they were, even if her actions were not directly connected to theirs.

I watched the three girls work out a scenario that included Ellen before they got down to playing. Their solution was that she would stay home and prepare her medicines and the equipment she used for her rescues while they were away on the adventure. Ellen had no problem with that and played in parallel with them, talking to herself and working dilgently in a small medical center she created for herself in what was usually the kitchen of the class playhouse.

Watching these three girls, and dozens of young (between the ages of four and eight) children over the past thirty years, I've been struck by the ease with which young children distinguish reality from controlled fantasy, and the naturalness they find in make-believe. They have no trouble putting the daily and ordinary world aside and imagining the laws of physics and personality as well as culturally sanctioned rules of normal behavior suspended or changed. They are often more relativistic and less rigid than the adults around them. In children's play, adults are often parodied, mocked, and turned into comic and pathetic characters who know little about life and possibility.

I've also seen the same youngsters, by the time they are thirteen or fourteen, begin to become like the adults they mocked at the same time they feel they are rejecting the culture and values of their parents. They are in the world, not just imagining what it would be like to be in it. Frequently they develop cynical attitudes toward the adult life around them. Fantasy plays a different role at this stage of development, mediating the passage from childhood to adulthood. Personal independence and family loyalty often come in conflict. This is the time of life when peer loyalty vies with family loyalty, and familial bonds are broken, creating friction in the family, a sense of abandonment by both parents and children, and a sadness in communal life, which can lead to permanent alienation.

The pull to be accepted by one's peers seems to overwhelm imagination and judgment for many young people between the ages of thirteen and sixteen in our society. The groups can range from a street gang to an evangelist church, from a cheerleading squad to a football team (there are gender-related sanctions that have powerful effects at these ages). What they have in common is the seductive power of group pressure and social rewards that suppress the private and the social imagination. Social and cultural mechanisms, often dominated by sanctioned media images of power and style, constrict the imagination during adolescence.

I remember the "music wars" of my three children and their friends during their junior and senior high school days. You had to like either country music, reggae, or rock. Classical music was out of the question in terms of informal student debate (sometimes conflict) at the school. It wasn't really a question of music but of who your friends were, how they identified themselves, and how you wanted to be perceived by them. In private, the kids, many of whom I worked with on literacy and theater projects, were open and gentle, curious about everything. In public, they engaged in battles, often over music: country versus rock; rock versus reggae; reggae versus country. One of the biggest challenges I faced those days as a parent and as a teacher was to create boundary crossings, to find ways for style to be replaced by substance and affection. I didn't succeed.

The tension between the imagination and conformity is central to the development of moral values. Imagination is usually characterized as the ability of the mind to form images, thoughts, melodies, or equations that are not present to the senses and have not been known or experienced in the past. It is the creative or constructive faculty of the human mind. The imagination gives rise to the idea of possibility, and to the contrast between what is and what might be. The power of the imagination comes from our ability to entertain alternatives to what we have experienced or have been told. The existence of imagination is perhaps the originating force of the ideas of freedom, choice, and the possibility of personal, social, and political change. If we were not able to imagine the world as other than it is, then change in which we take an active role would be unthinkable. To locate change and possibility within a choosing person is to attribute to the imagination the ability to envision transformations of the world and motivate people to act upon them.

Our concept of time, and in particular the future, may be a product of our ability to imagine. In our society (with the exception of people who believe in complete predestination), we consider the future as a realm of possibility, and act as if we had the ability to make choices that can determine to some degree how the future will turn out. By valuing the imagination, we empower ourselves to dream of the world becoming a better or more decent place, which provides an opening for us to act to transform it. When we give up to fate, destiny, or the power of others our imagination, possible worlds close down.

At moments in my life I have felt my imagination soar and new possibilities for living and acting opened up. These times set me out on paths that have defined the moral quality of my life. For example, I remember when I was about eight or nine sitting around the kitchen table at my grandparents' apartment. It must have been 1945 or '46, and my grandfather's union was out on strike. The strike must have been going on for a while, because the people sitting around the table were depressed; it was hard to feed their families and keep up their loan payments while being out on strike. One of the men was crying. His wife was sick, they had a new baby, he couldn't pay the heating bill and was worried about their ability to survive the strike. Everyone had a sad and wrenching story, and I felt like crying, too. My grandfather passed around a bottle of Canadian Club, getting people to pledge help to one another and share what little they had, and then telling them stories about what the world could be like for workers. His stories were told in a mixture of Yiddish and English, and I could only make out their bare outlines. But from the tone and nature of the conversation it seemed that they warmed up everyone at the table as much as the whiskey did. The storytelling itself inspired me as much as the vision of a decent and just future worth struggling for that it conjured up. What I got from that evening and many others like it listening to my grandfather was a sense of the power of stories and of imagining good things in hard times, of keeping hope alive and never believing that "reality" was fixed once and for all. Over the years I have learned how to tell stories, too, and believe that much of my work has been devoted to keeping hope alive during hard times.

Of course the imagination is not always so benign a power.

As much as we have the power to imagine the world as better, we also have the power to imagine it as worse. There are children, even as young as eight, who do not believe they will live beyond their twenties. They grow up on what Piri Thomas called "mean streets" and imagine their funerals rather than their futures. There are youngsters whose imaginations have been reduced to imagining "going out in style" by the age of twenty-four. This reduction of the imagination to its least possible denominator is a social, economic, and cultural phenomenon, but might also be a consequence of their not having alternative models or stories from a more hopeful world to fall back on.

In the imagination we can act out our own deaths, skewer and torture enemies, treat others as objects of our whim, create worlds in which decency is just a rumor. One of the central characteristics of the imagination is that it crosses borders and categories. It is, of itself, neither decent nor indecent, good nor evil. It has the power to posit the best and the worst of things, and to imagine things beyond moral judgment such as mathematical theorems, melodies, and machines.

The imagination crosses other borders as well. It is composed of thought and feeling but is not exclusively either. It is driven in part by the conscious mind, and in part by the ruminations of the unconscious. It plays freely but is also determined by what we have experienced. It can be comic or tragic, melodramatic or just silly. It is, in a way, an internal voyager accessible to all people who have not had their minds and spirits destroyed. It makes a person bigger than her or his experience and is the strongest manifestation of the idea of freedom that we know on an intimate level.

From one perspective, the imagination is the power to go beyond experience and, in the mind, break or change the rules of all the games we are forced to play, whether they are imposed by other people, genetics, or the natural world. It is a source of new rules as well, of thinking the as yet unthought as we experiment with the development of felt values.

From another perspective the imagination can be seen as the basis of all experience in the young child. It is out of the spectrum of the possible presented by the imagination that the child selects and constructs the "real." The world, looked at in this way, emerges from experiences that inform, shape, and limit the imagination. What is real is negotiated and constructed, and though there is a common core of agreed upon reality, the rest of our vision of what is real flows over the borders of the imagination.

When looking at the child's vision of the world, and listening to the imaginative play of children, the permeability of reality, its amorphous edges, becomes clear. And when children experiment with moral values, their constricted worlds, including all of the preachings and actions of their parents and the other people around them, are subject to the scrutiny and transformative powers of the imagination. It is for that reason that it is crucial to look closely at the imagination at play in the child's world if one is to understand the transformation of experience and imaginings into value and moral principle.

So far I've described an instance of children's collective imagining. Andrea, Ellen, and Sasha created an imaginary world in which all three of them participated. However, imaginings can take place in solitude as well as in a group. My own children, as well as many youngsters I've taught, animate dolls and stuffed animals and enter into imagined worlds, talking with and through these vehicles for projecting character and personality. That play also involves two levels of conversation: talking the plot to oneself, and entering into the plot and being a part of the action. I've noticed that such solitary play often begins with a child addressing her or his toys or dolls and inviting them to play before the play actually begins. Statements directed to particular toys, such as, "Let's play today," or, "Do you want to play with me today?" often precede play. They seem to provide a ritual entrance into the world of the imagination and a conscious suspension of the rules and conventions of ordinary living.

The decision to shift into an imaginative mode is often a conscious one for children. They know they are playing, though sometimes the play world becomes so convincing during the play that they lose sight of the conventions and control they begin with. Young children talk their way into imaginary play and often narrate the action, at least until momentum develops. There seems to be dual consciousness involved in imaginative play: the play that is fully absorbing, and at the same time the narrative control of the play that is based on a child's conscious awareness that she or he is playing. This dual character of spontaneity and control is characteristic of the way in which the workings of the imagination cross boundaries and categories.

The balance between control and spontaneity in play varies with different forms of play. Sometimes children control the plots of their play in ritualistic ways: dolls have to be placed in particular poses, obey formal rules of adult behavior, and repeat former instances of similar play down to the smallest gesture and act. Tea parties and dinner parties can be played out almost identically over and over. The rituals of dressing Barbie dolls and going to proms can be regularized as can be war games with GI Joe and adventures with plastic horses. Other times, spontaneity can be dominant and the control of play loosened. At those times children seem to plunge into plots with no idea where they'll come out and sometimes will end up with all their toys scattered about, any sense of linear plot lost in all the little side actions and explorations that developed along the way.

Children enjoy both forms of play, though too often adults prefer to see their children playing in orderly and structured ways, and spontaneity and wildness is suppressed. I believe this is a major mistake. One has to learn to live within rule-governed behavior and also learn to function when the rules no longer hold. Wild play—explorations without the guide of set plots and predictable rituals—is as much a preparation for life as is controlled play.

Sometimes it is difficult to know how consciously children control the plots they play. I've seen what could be called run-away play, where what seems to be fairly ritualized play gets out of hand. For example, there were a number of boys and girls in a kindergarten class I taught who loved to build a great big raft out of blocks and other scraps of wood we had in the class-room. The children built the raft on the rug of the storytelling and group learning center in the room, which took up over a third of the classroom. Usually about a dozen children played at sailing out to sea and having a stormy lost-at-sea adventure. The children would usually talk out the outlines of the play sit-uation while they built the raft, choosing roles for themselves and letting one another know what characters were in the game. I used to marvel at how elaborate and multifocused the children's adventures were. They might discover an uninhab-ited island, or run into a pirate ship, or find themselves discov-ering a lost continent. Many of the adventures had echoes of myths and stories they had encountered at home, on TV, or in the classroom.

There would usually be a captain and crew who went about navigating the ship and managing to get through a storm or rough seas oblivious to all of the little dramas that took place on board during the passage. Then there were animal families on board, children running away from home, pirates who robbed rich people who then turned around and chased the pirates and had mock battles with them. These adventures usually took place before lunch, and when I wasn't using that time to tutor an individual or work with a small group, I loved to step back and watch the development of such complex, polyrhythmic, and multistranded play.

It took me a while to trust that things wouldn't get out of hand, and that's how I came to understand the important role of the children's initial setting of themes, characters, and plots. This second-level narrative set the ground rules for the play, allowed the children to know what to expect, and gave them the trust to let loose and enter the imaginary worlds they created. As I mentioned above, there were a few times when this complex play exploded and I had to intervene and rescue the situation from chaos. Once, one of the pirates tripped over a block and fell on top of the captain who was navigating through a particularly perilous rocky landscape. The captain exploded, a fight began, and the children and blocks went tumbling all over the room. I quickly engineered a story time and also managed to get the children to clean up before lunch. There was no one to blame, and I let the children know how impressive their play usually was, and asked them what went wrong. One of the children simply said the crew and the pirates weren't supposed to play together. The others agreed that it wasn't in the story, that that was not the way things were set up. I agreed it was an accident, and that was that. What struck me was how so many of the children understood that the rules they had set up for their own play had been accidently violated, and that they hoped I wouldn't prohibit such games simply because things went wrong one time. For the children, this wild and improvised play was hedged in and protected by rules, narratives, story lines, and character definitions—by the parameters they'd agreed upon within which their imaginations could have free and relatively safe rein.

The direction of children's imaginative play is often quite consciously controlled by the players who make decisions about the structure of the plot or adventure and the use of props and playthings. The processes that occur during imaginative play represent the emergence of the ability to think about what one is doing at the same time as being engaged in the action—that is the emergence of reflection and speculation about the meaning and value of action. This reflexive thinking is central to the development of the ability to think through complex moral situations, weigh values, make conscious choices, and take responsibility for one's actions.

A child's growth takes place within a particular situation not of her or his choosing. That situation is determined by economic, social, cultural, and moral factors. Nobody clues the child in on many of the circumstances that affect the everyday behavior of parents, teachers, and other people in the environment. Children are often left to figure out what is happening around them, what values are inherent in the other people in their worlds, and what choices they can safely make in the world as it is given to them. Because of the often complex and unarticulated structures that govern behavior, the imagination is a necessity in children's lives. They can figure out what is in their world only if they have the ability to think of the world as otherwise. There is a need to set up contrasts, to imagine differences in order to get at what seems to be going on. How does one make sense of one's parents' anger; of poverty or wealth; of an argument; of expressions of hatred or prejudice, or equally of love? The imagination has a lot to do during childhood. Meaning has to emerge from experience and the ability of the mind to explore possibilities—to imagine, for example, what an angry parent is like when he or she is not angry, or to imagine the persistence of love during hard times, is essential if one's world is not to fall apart.

I am not sure whether imaginative play with possible worlds is a universal feature of childhood. In fact, I believe that nobody has enough information to make any universal claims about the inner lives of all children. I wish to see all children as having full, imaginative play lives that allow them to transcend, if only in small ways, the accidents of birth and culture. It helps me retain hope for children who are starving or brutalized; for youngsters who are born into families who have no power or apparent hope in the world. It keeps open the possibility that the children will not die giving up on dreaming of a better world for themselves and their families. It also nurtures belief in the possibility of creating a decent world for all of its people. Yet I don't know the breadth and extent of the imaginative lives of children, nor understand fully the forces that kill the imagination and crush hope. I have not been able to figure out how children can grow into adults capable of killing or exploiting one another without concern or conscience. My intuition is that somewhere in the formula is an impoverishment or perversion of the imagination.

However, every once in a while there is some confirming voice, some unexpected evidence, that the imagination is an essential component of personhood, and that it actively resists suppression. One such confirmation can be found in Kornei Chukovsky's delightful children's book *From Two to Five*.[17] The book, originally published in 1925, was an attack on those people in the Soviet Union who advocated denying children access to fairy tales, nursery and nonsense rhymes, and all other forms of imaginative and nonrealistic stories. The idea behind this was that citizens of the new USSR, which was to be a totally planned and rational society, would be corrupted by the imagination. Chukovsky's book is an attack on such a total commitment to rational planning, and a celebration of the resilience of the child mind in the face of pressure to become mindless and obedient. One section illustrates the flavor of what child resistance to attempts to suppress the imagination might be like:

> Once upon a time there lived in Moscow a pedologist (an expert on child development) by the name of Shnchinskaia. And a very strange thing happened to this pedologist.
>
> She was also a mother, and she did everything in her power to protect her son from fairy tales. Even when she talked to him about animals she made sure to mention only those he had seen with his own eyes. After all, he had to grow up a realist . . .
>
> And everything would have been just fine, but, unfortunately, as a loving mother she began to keep a most detailed diary about her little son. Without being aware of it, she contradicted, in her entries, all her favorite arguments about the harmful influences of fantastic tales and destroyed them with her own pen . . .
>
> She wrote in this diary . . . that her boy, as if to make up for the fairy tales of which he had been deprived, began to spin from morning till night the wildest fantasies. He pretended that a red elephant came to live in his room; he invented a friend—a bear whom he named Cora; and he would often say, "Please, don't sit on the chair next to mine because—can't you see?—the she-bear is sitting on it." And, "Mother, why are you walking right on top of the wolves? Can't you see the wolves standing there?" . . .
>
> And although his mother observed that he literally bathed in fantasies as in a river, she continued to "protect" him from the ill effects of books of fairy tales.
>
> As if there were a basic difference between the fairy tale that a child made up himself and one that was created for him (as a folk tale) by imaginative folk or by a good writer. . . . Moreover, all his

playing is a dramatization of a fairy tale which he creates on the spot, animating, according to his fancy, all objects—converting any stool into a train, into a house, into an airplane, or into a camel. . . . In all this children become authors of and, at the same time, actors in fairy tales, expressing themselves in dramatic play. And their urge to believe in their imaginings is so strong that every attempt to put them into a frame of reality evokes a vigorous protest.[18]

The mother reminds me of many Christian fundamentalists who try to protect their children from "Satan's" fairy tales. I have had several adult students who grew up within such families and had since strayed a bit. They are still reverent and practicing Christians, but delight in fairy tales, fantasies, and imaginings. They often speak about how they learned to trust their imaginations in a context where the fear of imagining was an overriding obsession with their parents. I choose to believe, with Chukovsky, in the strength of childhood imaginings, and believe it is worth examining some of the ways in which they nurture growth. It is one of my working assumptions as an educator that, unless it can be proved otherwise, all children have the power of their imaginations as part of their birthright.

Recently I heard the most dramatic example of how the same imagination that enriches child life can at times be called on to nurture an adult living under intolerable circumstances. Berooz, an educator I have worked with, is Iranian and spent several years in jail, first under the Shah and then under the Khomeini regime. He told me that he was kept in solitary confinement for months at a time. The way he kept alive and sane was by imagining the music he loved, and following it note by note. He imagined classical Iranian music, Beethoven symphonies and operas, and reenacted in his mind plays he knew, creating imaginary sets and casts and performances in his head. He created elaborate stories and imagined writing them down, word by word. His imaginative life nurtured his spirit, and he was able to survive all of the attempts to torture thought, feeling, and hope out of him.

Jean Genet tells similar stories of his time in solitary confinement, of peopling his cell with imaginary beings whose lives he could play out in detail as a way of getting through days without light or contact with other human beings. He had to orient himself through the development of imaginative worlds, as there was no external stimulus.

One of the most vivid tales of the strength of childhood imagination is told in Gerald Vizenor's experiment in autobiography, *Interior Landscapes*. Vizenor, who is a mixed-blood Ojibwa, grew up in a difficult, marginal world of foster homes and temporary dwellings. His father was murdered when he was two years old, and his mother and her male friends moved in and out of his life throughout his childhood. Fortunately he had a grandmother who could tell him stories, inform him that he was a member of the crane people and a descendant of tricksters. Vizenor imagined tricksters, the flights of the crane, and felt part of a spiritual world that was accessible through his imagination. It helped him become a witness of his growing up rather than a victim of it. He could imagine the world as other, and in fact saw through the veil of his youthful experience in Minneapolis during the 1940s and '50s to the eternal trickster stories it recycled. Here is Vizenor talking about being nourished and nurtured by his trickster imagination in the third grade. Would that all of us could have such depth, grounding, and humor to draw on:

> Tribal tricksters arise in imagination, create the earth, chance, praise, impermanence, humorous encounters, and totems, and liberate the mind in their stories. The cranes endure these cre-

ations, these interior landscapes, and turn their voices to the seasons, the remembered seasons. . . .

Tricksters were my preparation for one more year in the third grade. The best world moved in stories at my desk that first year in silence, and then the crane arose in me and we celebrated tricksters on the margins. My dreams became stories; tricksters touched me at the windows, and tricksters overturned boredom, monotheism, coarse repetitions in the classroom, and lured me to the river. My tricksters raised me in imagination, and we were remembered in stories; we were wild, wild on the ice, wild banners on a winter bus at night in the cities.

These tricksters and woodland armies marched with me in the service and held me awake with humor as a military guard. The tricksters sat with me in stories, wavered with me in baronial museums, held me wild in ornamental grammars and untamed in heroic causes. Tricksters eased the pain in stories: when my elbow cracked on a stone, and a rope burned me to the wrist bone, when a relative died. Stories were told to measure lines and liberate my mind at school, at cafeterias, at the court house on probation, on road marches in the military, on the interstate, and at banks. The trickster has been a gambler, a priest, a translator, a poet, and a lover in some stories. . . .

The tricksters were with me in stories, and we remembered how to turn pain and horror into humor, how to distract the river mermen with language games and contradictions. Evangelists wounded our imagination and demanded our best humor, renunciation on the run; the tricksters and our stories liberated the mind. When those wicked warlocks promised the new world, the newer, and then the late world, their objective complements were overturned by woodland tricksters.[19]

The creation of imaginary worlds, possible plots and scenarios, as well as reflection on that play, is just one way that the ability to imagine things as different from how they are in everyday life is available to children. Listening to stories, for example, allows children to enter into other, often traditional, possible worlds where the constraints of ordinary life are transcended. The phrase "enter into" is not merely a metaphor: children seem to step into good stories and listen as if in a trance. Phrases like "Once upon a time" or "Long ago in a land far away" are ritualistic ways of informing children that reality is being suspended and fantasy is taking over. When I've taught kindergarten, story time was sacred. If someone came in and interrupted an absorbing story, the children would look up at the intruder as if they were awakened from a dream, and often chase them off. It seemed as if a violation of their inner space had occurred, some involuntary awakening from another world that they resented.

Stories have their appropriate levels of intimacy. Some are tales told to oneself, reflections on what one's life was or might be. Others are for the family or close friends. There are also contexts for some stories. When I was growing up, many of the older people told stories about Jews in Eastern Europe, stories that showed how even in the worst ghetto conditions, a good mind and patience could often triumph over brute force. These stories were about Jews for Jews. We never would have thought to tell them to our Italian or Irish neighbors, just as they would never tell us some of their most valued stories. The stories were about our survival as a group, about our sense of being at home with one another, and, most importantly, about using our wits to turn other people's prejudice against them rather than let it hurt us. For example, there are powerful and imaginative stories created within the community of enslaved African Americans during the time of slavery. They are about people who could fly and are remarkable tales of the free spirit and mind that, despite enslavement, protect one from accepting the role of a slave. They are also tales of escape and liberation, as accessible to five-year-olds as to adults. The stories are wonderful instances of the power of the imagination, as manifested in folktales, to allow people to transcend the material conditions of their lives and dream new and better worlds. The story of people who could fly is one of self-affirmation. It tells slaves that they come from a great people and must remember who they are and dream of what they can be. Their imaginations must take them beyond the present and accidental conditions of their lives and keep their minds "fixed on freedom." Virginia Hamilton retells many of these tales in her book *The People Could Fly*.[20]

Powerful and imaginative stories have a way of surviving over time and finding new life under changed circumstances. *The People Could Fly* celebrates the spirits who had the strength to flee slavery and teaches about the inner preparation that precedes the physical act of risking one's life for freedom. While there is no more institutionalized slavery in the United States, much of the substance of slavery (such as economic dependency) is perpetuated through racism and the violence of poverty that still characterize life in the U.S. for many African American people. The need to fly away from racist oppression in order to develop a full and free life persists, and therefore the need for stories about freedom and the strength of the imagination to overcome depression and despair is as strong as ever. Not surprisingly, therefore, stories of flying people have been revived and retold. Virginia Hamilton's retelling speaks to the liberation of the spirit and the resulting struggle for actual and physical liberation.

The artist and storyteller Faith Ringgold has transformed the tale into a moving and inspiring story for young children in her book *Tar Beach*.[21] The central character in the story, an eight-year-old, tells us toward the beginning of the book that she can fly, and that means she's free to go anywhere.

In the course of the book, Cassie tells us how she is going to make her father rich and stop her mother from crying all winter over the frustrations and humiliations her husband goes through because he can't get into the union and have a decent job. Cassie also tells us how she'll make sure the family gets ice-cream desserts for dinner and even agrees to teach her brother how to fly. At the end of the book she addresses the reader and says that anyone can fly if there is a place you need to be and there's no other way to get there. It is an affirmation of the imagination and the power of young people to act in the world.

I have read this book with five- and six-year-olds, and they all loved Cassie. Some had problems that were similar to hers; others had their own forms of wanting to grow beyond the worlds they were born into. They understood the metaphor of flying as an image of their own potential freedom. The affirmative power of the imagination, the ability to envision the world other than it is, is directly at the heart of childhood and nurtures growth under the most difficult of circumstances.

However it's not all happy endings when it comes to imaginative life. The imagination can be redeeming and nurturing. It can also be used as an instrument for plotting revenge, scheming up mischief, and indulging in fantasies of violence and domination. The imagination is not itself moral, but it allows one to entertain possible moralities and immoralities. It provides a moderately safe way to test out guesses and hints about what is right and wrong, and develop ideas about what one deserves from life and ought to give to life. It provides a palette with which one can paint possible values, and safely imagine oneself to be a saint or a devil. This is particularly true of children whose play is often a complex mix of goodness, wickedness, and a playful testing of the limits of power.

Recently I observed a group of three- and four-year-olds playing together at a friend's house. We adults were sitting around the central room of the house talking while the children played. The room was a combined dining room, kitchen, living room, and child's playroom, as well as a guest bedroom. Therefore, there were a lot of little corners and different environments for the children to use for their play, and they took full advantage of the space. I noticed in the course of several hours that their play ranged from spanking dolls to rescuing toy horses, and included building and destroying towers and forts, and almost too gleefully tearing apart an already broken doll, saying it was dead. They took the doll outside and may have buried it reverently or burned it gleefully. Though I didn't know what happened with the doll, I did see them go after the family cat in the same way and try to harm it. Fortunately, cats can take care of themselves, and the children's attempts to dismember it led to their being scratched. Their actions horrified us but led to some complex and difficult conversations with the children. Fantasy cruelty borders perilously close to cruelty in the actual world, and children needed to be made aware of that.

The imagination reaches into and beyond the forbidden and the unspoken. It is possible to break all moral principles in one's imagination, and to create new ones that make the most unlikely demands upon behavior and good sense. Children move easily in the plastic environment of the imagination, and it has always surprised me how simpleminded most adult schemes about the moral development of children are, given the complex imaginary lives children lead. There seems to be an adult tendency toward simplification that filters out ambiguity, fantasy, wildness, and wickedness, as well as the many manifestations of generosity and compassion that children demonstrate in their play and storytelling. Perhaps a main reason for such underestimation of the child's ability to function in many, often contradictory, imaginative worlds simultaneously is that such flexibility and creativity calls into question the ability of adults to legislate or teach morals. If one accepts the centrality of the imagination and its power to make all values thinkable, then there is no way to control the imaginative moral experiments children make, or predict the values they will emerge with and be willing to act upon.

There is an unfortunate tendency in our culture to separate thought and feeling, cognition and affect, and try to study one in isolation from the other. Howard Gardner, in his book *The Mind's New Science,* provides an account of "the cognitive revolution" of the 1950s, the separation between thinking and feeling that was part of a strategy in the development of the new cognitive sciences to choose to do research that will produce modest, reliable results and leave complex human issues to the future, when the methodology of cognitive science has been refined. Gardner lists, as one of the characteristics of cognitive science,

> the deliberate decision to de-emphasize certain factors which may be important for cognitive functioning but whose inclusion at this point would unnecessarily complicate the cognitive-scientific enterprise. These factors include the influence of affective factors or emotions, the contribution of historical and cultural factors, and the role of the background context in which particular actions or thoughts occur.[22]

The imagination cannot, however, be studied or understood in such a fragmentary way. It is of a whole: thought, feeling, play with images, the development of plot and character, and flirtation with experience on the margins of consciousness. The imagination is best thought of holistically, as a mode of mental functioning that disregards the conventions of ordinary experience and accepts itself as not representing the everyday physical and social world. Eduardo Galeano, in *The Book of Embraces,* introduces a new word, *"sentipensante,"* which applies to imaginative activity:

> Why does one write, if not to put one's pieces together? From the moment we enter school or church, education chops us into pieces: it teaches us to divorce soul from body and mind from heart. The fishermen of the Colombian Coast must be learned doctors of ethics and morality, for they invented the word *sentipensante,* feeling-thinking, to define language that speaks the truth.[23]

The imagination is *sentipensante.* It does not speak the truth, but allows people to play with possible truths, to transcend everyday reality and, through thought and feeling merged, begin to define and understand their own values. Interestingly enough, thought and feeling merged in imaginative play or reverie can at times suspend the laws of logic and reason, and even take a cold, neutral stance toward violence and other conceivable horrors, and at other times push logic and reason to cruel ends or manifest great compassion. Both thought and feeling are elements that can be played with within the realm of the imagination and, at the same time, be used to weigh and balance the values that emerge from these imaginative worlds.

Marie, one of my recent college students, is a Cambodian immigrant who experienced several years of slavery in a Khmer Rouge prison camp before she was ten, several more years in a refugee camp, and about ten years living in near poverty among hostile and racist people in the United States. Marie is never-theless one of the gentlest, most perceptive, and caring people I know, and paradoxically one of the most hopeful. She dreams of teaching children in the United States about democracy so they will realize what a precious thing it is and be able to live it. She has told me that since she has lived in the U.S. she has been spat at for being Asian, called names she refuses to repeat, been discriminated against at the university (a fact I can vouch for), and seen her parents treated as subhuman. At the same time, she has learned how to discover decent people, something she once told me you have to work hard at because so many people in the U.S. express affection loosely and without thought, and then use and throw away one another with no regard or re-spect.

I asked Marie how she survived the Khmer Rouge as a child and how she survived the initial disappointments of her hopes in the United States. She told me that, while very young, she learned how to read and how to tell stories. In the midst of the most enslaving work in the Khmer Rouge camps, in the midst of the forest when she tried to escape, in the refugee camps and in the basement apartment she lived in when she first came to the U.S., she imagined other worlds where she lived and thought through the specifics of what they would be like. She did not just feel her way into a new life but used her imagination to think her way into it as well. She said she could imagine in Cambodia fleeing from the Khmer Rouge. She imagined places she would be safe, down to the details where she would be sleeping, and forced herself to imagine the books she might have read. She thought and felt her way into other possible realities without denying the everyday horrors—there was no way for her to do that and remain sane. But by thinking and feeling her way into these imaginings, she said she kept herself from hating everybody and even life itself. She imagined another truth, another life, and after she graduated from college, she hoped to be able to build part of it for herself and the children she taught. She is teaching now, and writing, and I've found the quality of her imagination and will, and the strength of her decency, inspiring.

I once asked her how she kept all of her thoughts and imaginings together with her knowledge of everyday life, and wondered if she ever separated her feelings from them just to get by. She told me that the separation of thought and feeling, the management of life through the elimination of feeling when things got uncomfortable, was one thing she found in common between the Khmer Rouge and the people who controlled other people's lives in the United States. She felt that keeping her feelings and thoughts alive, and not retreating from the pain but living through it in her imagination, were what kept her from being bitter and hateful. She never forgot that things could be otherwise, and she nurtured this understanding. It has kept hope alive in her life and helped her become a caring and wise person whose dream is to remake the world rather than retreat from it or destroy it.

Not all young people have the imaginative and personal strength of Marie. Sometimes a young person gets too far into despair, and the imagination becomes morbid. Perhaps a story might have been of use, or a joke, or a loving touch; maybe a little fantasy about a possible beautiful world. But it is difficult to know the dynamics of the imagination of a silent child or one who gives up on life because imagination is no longer connected with life.

It is likely that every person who commits suicide has imagined her or his nonexistence. At moments, imagined nonexistence can become so attractive that it is embraced. It's possible that a day or even a moment later that seductive imagined release from pain and trouble would no longer have the power to cause a person to embrace death. A dear friend of mine changed her mind about suicide moments too late.

This poem, which was given to a teacher in Regina, Saskatchewan, by a twelfth grader, re-creates what I imagine a suicide's embrace of death might feel like. Although it is not known if this young man wrote the poem, it is known that he committed suicide a few days later. The poem originally appeared in *Generation* magazine.

He always wanted to explain things, but no one cared.
Sometimes he would draw and it wasn't anything.
He wanted to carve it in stone or write it in the sky.
He would lie out in the grass and look up in the sky
And it would only be him and the sky and the things
    inside him that needed saying.
And it was after that he drew the picture.
He kept it under his pillow and would let no one see
    it.
And he would look at it every night and think about it.
And when it was dark, and his eyes were closed, he
    could still see it.
And it was all of him. And he loved it.
When he started school he brought it with him.
Not to show anyone, but just to have it with him like a
    friend.
It was funny about school.
He sat in a Square, brown desk
Like all other square, brown desks.
And he thought it should be red.
And his room was a square, brown room
Like all the other rooms.
And it was tight and close. And stiff.
He hated to hold the pencil and chalk.

With his arm stiff and his feet flat on the floor, stiff.
With the teacher watching and watching.
The teacher came and spoke to him.
She told him to wear a tie like all the other boys.
He said he didn't like them.
She said it didn't matter.
After that they drew.
And it was all yellow and it was the way he felt about
 that morning.
And it was beautiful.
The teacher came and smiled at him.
"What's this?" she said. "Why don't you draw like
 Ken's drawing?
Isn't that beautiful?"
After that his mother bought him a tie.
And he always drew airplanes and rocketships like
 everyone else.
And he threw the old picture away.
And when he lay alone looking at the sky,
It was big and blue and all of everything,
But he wasn't anymore.
He was square inside, and brown.
And his hands were stiff.
And he was like everyone else.
And the thing inside him that needed saying didn't
 need it anymore.
It had stopped pushing
It was crushed. Stiff.
Like everything else.[24]

The simple ending to this essay is a plea for the creative, compassionate, and social imagination. We cannot afford to allow people to become so small that they can dream only a world of violence, greed, and joyless competition. Teachers and parents and all the rest of us need to be as imaginative as our children, to nurture their imaginations as well as our own, and to keep on, no matter the circumstances, dreaming and acting for a more decent, compassionate, and equitable world. In hard times, this is one of the finest gifts we can provide for our children, for other people's children, and for ourselves.

4.
Topsy-Turvies:
Teacher Talk and Student Talk

Opposition is true friendship.[25]
                          —William Blake

From things that differ come the fairest
attunement.
                          —Heraclitus

Teacher talk and student talk are essential components that determine the quality of learning in the classroom. When there is dissonance between them, other kinds of strife develop. When I first began teaching, I didn't know how to speak to or with my students. Standing in front of a group of young people is a linguistic challenge. It is not merely a matter of what you say but of how your language is understood and how you understand the language of your students. It is not just a matter of how you present lessons or counsel your students. Language is an every-day, every-minute matter, and nuances of inflection, tone, modulation, and vocabulary are constantly at play in the interaction of students and teachers. There is an unarticulated linguistic sensibility that determines the nature and quality of interaction in the classroom. Teachers are listened to more than they usually think they are, though listening, understanding, and obeying are three different things altogether.

When I was teaching a combined kindergarten and first grade in Berkeley, one of the students kept her face turned away from me during class discussions. I waited for a moment when Julia and I could talk privately and asked her what was wrong—was I too loud or were there other problems in the class—and her response was that she was afraid of not knowing the right answer to a question even if she knew it. She said she was afraid of my questions. Perhaps she was equally afraid of what she imagined to be my response.

This shocked me because I felt that I had created an open and giving environment where questions and answers could be seen as acts of exploration. I even had a sign on the wall proclaiming MAKE MISTAKES and encouraged the students to make interesting guesses without worrying about being correct. She had heard all of that but didn't believe me. School was about being right, and if you weren't right, you'd be punished. And worse, you could never know if you were right. It was up to what the teacher decided. It wasn't me who was making her face turn away, but the very idea of school performance, of having to expose her knowledge or lack of it in front of the other children in the class. She didn't know where she would come out and was afraid to find out.

For Julia it was not a question of being wrong but of never being sure in the presence of a teacher and classmates how you will look and whether you will be humiliated. I told her—and it took a while for her to accept it—that intelligent guessing was more important than avoidance of learning.

In a way, the story has two happy endings. Later that school year the class had to take the California Test of Basic Skills. One question on the test showed a woman mopping the floor. The question was: She likes to: a) cop, b) hop, c) mop, and d) pop. Julia and the rest of the girls in the class refused to answer the question, informing me that she does not like to mop. They could read. But they rejected the premises of the questions. And they felt that truth was stronger than testing. They were six years old.

What was I to do? Every one of those girls could read the question and knew the answer expected of them, but because of our discussions on women's rights, their own family's commitment to women's liberation, and their own perceptions that women do not like to mop, they had decided not to answer a question designed by so-called experts in phonics. You might say that the students had said, phonics be damned.

My problem was not to coerce the students into answering a question against their own conscience. I couldn't bring myself to do that. Rather it was whether to give them credit for an answer that I knew they could give if they chose to. It was a question of whether I should let them be punished for their own sensibilities or just fill in the right blank for them. If I did, would I be cheating for my students, or would they be cheated by the nature of the test and the budding sophistication of their social awareness if I didn't do it?

Ultimately I decided to give them credit. Knowledge and intelligence are more important than conformity to the norms of testing. And the sensible revolt of young children when they are articulate and clear about the issue is a sign of the success of education, not its failure.

The second happy ending is that Julia and the other girls in the class are doing very well now that they are in their thirties. This one question on a high-stakes test was not important, but talking to some of them I've learned that the support they received, the validation of their thoughts and ideas, and the defiance of unreasonable authority have stood them well over the years. School is a place of anxiety and strife for most students, and achieving the fairest attunement that Heraclitus refers to is a complex matter involving language, patience, visceral perception, intuition, intelligence, and compassion. On a minute-to-minute basis in the classroom, language is central to the development of attunement.

Recently I was asked to sit in on a classroom for a few hours in the hope that I could provide some insights into why the teacher was having trouble with students learning and even paying attention. The teacher was young, highly motivated, and committed, even passionate, about his students learning. Sitting in the back of a classroom when doing observations often has advantages. The children who'll be closest to you are the ones who either chose to sit in the back or were sent there. They are either the most indifferent or the most defiant. It's the cynical section of the seating arrangement. In the midst of the lesson, one of the back-of-the-roomers turned to another and said, "There he goes again." The other just shrugged and put his head on the desk.

My response was to listen more carefully to how the teacher was talking. He was young and inexperienced, and he had not developed a tone or manner in the classroom that was easy and sincere. He was playing at being a teacher, speaking the way he imagined teachers should talk, looking above the heads of his students, not making eye contact, and pushing on with the lesson, whether the students were understanding what he said or not. It was a function of his insecurity, though unfortunately he saw it as the students' inability to pay attention. He needed what I have come to call a topsy-turvy.

It is easy to create a topsy-turvy. Draw a circle with two parallel arcs in it, as in Figure 1. Then add some circles in the middle, and you have instant eyes and a face. Looked at one way, it

Figure 1.   Figure 2.   Figure 3.

is sad. Rotate it 180 degrees and it becomes happy. This is a simple topsy-turvy.

Topsy-turvies are illustrations that, when turned 180 degrees, display two completely different images. For example, a topsy-turvy might look like a smiling woman from one perspective, but when turned 180 degrees it might look like a nasty and angry pirate. It takes a lot of skill to make a convincing topsy-turvy. I have found that the concept of topsy-turvy provides a powerful metaphor that helps teachers transform their way of looking at themselves in the classroom. It is a matter of learning how to analyze the presentation of yourself in the classroom and then making a 180-degree shift and attempting to construct how your students see you. This implies an acceptance of opposition, of the idea that what you want as a teacher and what your students want or expect may be dissonant. It also requires the more personal and, in many ways, difficult integration of the idea that how you think you are speaking and how your students interpret what you are saying are not necessarily the same. The hard thing is talking to a whole class when people listen differently. Students interpret, reflect, analyze, and respond to the nuances of language in the classroom, and since most of the permitted language in the classroom is teacher talk, it is to that language that an excessive amount of student emotion and intelligence is committed.

It is essential to realize that this is not a matter of lack of caring or the will to help students. It is more a question of social and linguistic differences in a context where students and teachers are not hearing language in the same way. It is not just teacher talk that is problematic. Student talk has to be interpreted as well. This has nothing to do with language differences. It has everything to do with the way in which language is heard and interpreted, with tone, presentation, attitude, implication, and an understanding of how to convey complex meaning in a way that is understood by the spoken-to. It is essentially a question of trying to understand what students are saying in a context where teachers are not accustomed to listening and students are not accustomed to speaking openly and honestly in school.

This places a burden on teachers who are supposed to be the authorities in the classroom. The exchange of ideas, feelings, social understanding, and conversation in the classroom is fundamentally under the control of teachers unless the classroom is out of control. This is independent of teaching styles and pedagogical orientation. Language exists not merely on the level of words, sentences, paragraphs, dialects, accents, and linguistic differences. It is a social phenomenon that has complex personal implications relating to how the more formal aspects of reading, writing, and talking are interpreted on an everyday basis. It has to do with how things are said, how questions are asked or answered, and how much teachers and students listen to one another.

New teachers, if they do not come from communities that are similar to those they teach in, are particularly vulnerable to miscommunication. The students do not yet know or understand their teachers' style of talking. The teachers don't know how they are being heard. There is a lot of literature about learning style but not enough about teaching language and styles. The presentation of self in the classroom is a major part of the effectiveness of connecting with students and enhancing their learning. If you are too soft, too hard, too rigid, or too permissive, the students will become confused and often will feel alienation from the culture of the classroom. It is a short step from this sense of alienation to the development of hostility or resistance to learning within the classroom. Casual remarks can become defining moments in your relationship with your class.

Over the past few years I have seen teachers tell students how much they love them and then have found out that some of them didn't know all of their students' names. Young people are experts at understanding false pretensions of love and caring. After all, it's hard to love someone you don't really know. And if you say you love your students, you can be sure that they will test that protestation of affection.

Recently I visited a classroom where the children were out of control. I found them imaginative and ingenious in their strategies of defiance, but found myself angry at them. I didn't love what they were doing to themselves, and felt they had developed dysfunctional school behavior that would end up hurting them in the future. The teacher, a very caring but inexperienced person, was screaming love at the children, saying how wonderful they were and how much she cared about them. Their response was cynical defiance and mockery. They were in control while they were out of control.

I visited another classroom where the teacher took the opposite tack and applied heavy and punitive discipline. The students' response was the same. There is a fine line between discipline and love that leads to good learning and creative teaching. "Tough love" makes no sense to me. The line I am

107

talking about has to do with creating trust, respect, and a sense of teacherly identity. For, as a teacher, it is essential to be an adult among young people. This may sound trivial or silly, because it is hard to know what it means to be an adult. For me it has to do with passionate and loving authority and knowledge. You have to know what you are teaching, to learn how to understand your students both as individuals and as a group, and to fight against resistance to learning. You are not one of them, and you are being paid; they are required to attend. Teaching is a matter of craft, experience, and art, which makes it a continuing challenge to teach well. A teacher's language and the nature of the conversation in his or her classroom are determining factors in learning.

This implies that teachers should be aware of the major challenge of understanding how they are heard and not merely concentrating on how students speak and respond to teacher speech. Consciousness of the listener is hardly attended to in teacher education. It requires a topsy-turvy, an attempt to pay attention to how you are heard at the same time you are talking. Lovers do this all of the time. They speak to each other and worry about whether they are understood. Politicians do the same thing. They speak in order to win an audience, and if they are not conscious about how they are being understood, they will lose their audience. The same thing is true for actors in live theater, where sensitivity to the audience helps shape the intensity and effectiveness of a performance.

Teaching is performance. It doesn't make a difference whether you are teaching in a structured, full-frontal teaching classroom or in a personalized environment where there is opportunity to work with students individually or in small groups. The way in which a teacher speaks shapes students' attitudes and is a major determinant in the nature and quality of the learning environment.

Small things—comments, questions, responses, phrases, tone—often make big differences in student attitudes, not merely toward their teachers, but toward what their teachers teach. Over the past few years I've been observing a number of young teachers in their classrooms. I know the students' and teachers' behavior were affected by my presence, but not enough to conceal the nature of life and culture of the classrooms. What has been striking is the covert language of the children and the struggles the teachers have to be taken seriously by their students. One dramatic example was in a fourth-grade classroom. The teacher, a young man with high motivation, love of children, and no experience living or working with children of color from poor communities, was struggling to give the class a homework assignment. About twelve of the twenty-five students paid attention—that was the core of the class that did the work he assigned and often found themselves oppressed and harassed by other students who found the entire academic enterprise of the classroom irrelevant to their lives. Given his commitment to the learning of all of the students, he rephrased the assignment, diagrammed it on the chalkboard, and handed out clear instructions that a few of the recalcitrant students made into paper airplanes and threw around the classroom.

At last, in a fit of anger caused by the frustration of not being able to teach or help people he knew needed his help, he exploded at one of the boys in the room. At that point, another boy, clearly a leader, said, "Okay, Mr. Gold, we'll let you talk."

The students were aware of how the teacher was struggling to find a presence and language adequate to the authority the school district had vested in him. It was a dysfunctional topsy-turvy—teacher authority and student power. The authority was neglected, the power misused. The students knew they were in control of language in the classroom. There were linguistic as well as psychological and social conflicts between teacher and students, all within the context of a school without a commitment to nurturing its students or teachers and with no vision of learning beyond getting the school average on high-stakes tests as high as they could manufacture.

What struck me was that this student had understood that he and other students in the class controlled the language in the classroom. He knew how to pay no attention to what the teacher said. This, of course, meant that he understood that the teacher, a very caring young man, was out of his element. He was teaching students from communities that he had not grown up in, students who had had bad experiences in previous schools, who had no reason to trust him, and, most of all, who had given up on learning. This, of course, wasn't true for all of the students in the class. It was painful to see the serious students trying to deal with the sophisticated, often violent, subversion that they and their teacher had to suffer from other students.

Recently I observed another painful situation, one that I have faced over the years. I was not as tender as Francisa, who had come from a middle-class Latino family and had had to deal with complex questions of racism, curriculum, and respect. She didn't know that all of these things are intimately bound in a complex fabric where you can pull out one thread and the whole thing will disintegrate. It was about 1:45 in the afternoon. The sixth-grade class had begun at 1:20 (schools have crazy time schedules, which I have never figured out but accept when I observe classrooms). I believe the subject was creating a family history and learning about the history of the community you live in. Things were going along well—about half of the students were interested in the project, and the others were passive or asleep. The pain of seeing 50 percent of the kids disappearing in the classroom, something I have experienced more than any person should have to witness, was depressing me. There were kids who were doing what the teacher wanted or were just fading into their fantasies of life after and outside of schools.

An African American student walked in halfway through the class, threw his duffel bag under his seat, punched a Latino student who was sitting in what he assumed was a chair that was his, and took over the space.

I waited for the teacher's response.

Nothing.

Nothing.

Who was being damaged? Both students and the teacher who was out of contact with the children she was teaching. My instincts told me she was afraid of them. There was no one at the school to support her. She was young and romantic yet had no connection to the community and didn't understand how tough it can be to teach children who don't know or trust you.

The question of building trust and developing comfort is not usually a part of teacher education, and the mismatch between young teachers and the communities they serve is endemic and too often unarticulated.

The student who had tossed his bag under the desk had come in with an attitude, and was at least a half hour late for the class. All of the other kids looked at the teacher, since she had to deal with his comments on everything she said while she was trying to teach. My temptation was to intervene, but at that moment it would have undermined her authority. For me, she had the feel, intelligence, and touch that would make for wonderful teaching after three or four years of struggle.

I kept quiet and watched. The class went on, and finally she reached the point where she told the boy to shut up. A number of the girls in the class, all African American and Latino, just about cheered. But he turned to her and said, "Are you a racist? Do you hate black people?"

Francisa had a panicked look on her face. She didn't consider herself an overt racist, had studied racism and its manifestations in an elite college, had a keen sense of racial and social conflict in the United States, and fell into the trap. "Yes," she said, "all non-black people are racist, and I have had to deal with my own racism."

All of that may be true, and it's a complex issue that young teachers have to deal with in an everyday and personal way. But when? and where? and how? Is it a matter for classroom discourse? Or does it expose you to a student who knows your vulnerabilities, takes you off your center, and makes teaching and maintaining a disciplined and compassionate educational community in the classroom impossible?

This new teacher was in a classroom of eleven- and twelve-year-olds, not in a semiotics or sociology class in college. Her language created hostility and rage she could not have anticipated and was not prepared to work with. Schools are not colleges, and students don't always have the reverence for grades or their professors that many of their teachers have had when they got their credentials. It is essential to understand that many schools and classrooms in the poorest communities in our society are run, on a social and emotional level, by the students and not by the teachers. The language in the classroom is a negotiation between teachers and students, with the students often having the power. That is not usually understood when classroom practice is planned or evaluated. You mess with the kids and you simply will not survive, and that includes white middle-class kids as well as children who have the misfortune to come from families that are under economic stress.

The all-too-frequent disconnect between students and

teachers often hangs on words and inflections. Put one student down or humiliate her or him in front of the other students and a complex ambiance of disrespect has been created.

I remember my first revolt as a student. It was in 1949, at junior high school P.S. 82 in the Bronx. I was in a combined seventh- and eighth-grade class. We had a wonderful teacher who was known and loved in the community. She retired in the middle of the school year and was replaced by a young teacher who was clearly motivated but inexperienced. The class, all of us, were either Jewish or Italian, and in those days, the recovery from World War II, the Holocaust, and the struggle to create the state of Israel were in everyone's mind every day. The teacher was neither Jewish nor Italian, and definitely was not a New Yorker. I can still see her face and still feel guilt about what happened to her.

Her first goal was to shape us up. But we were a gifted class, and we didn't need any shaping up. Her second goal was to keep us quiet. But anyone who has ever tried to teach Jewish and Italian kids knows that silence is not part of our culture. The third goal was to erase the memory of our retired teacher, which was a major strategic mistake. You celebrate the memory of people who are loved and try to move in their jet stream until you find your own way. Then you become an honored member of the community and can mobilize support.

However, this teacher started out by telling us how much more discipline oriented she would be, how she would make us work harder, would not tolerate informal conversation in the classroom and, most of all, "would not let you people bring your cultural politics into the classroom."

In Jewish communities, when someone says "you people," it feels, smells, and sounds like anti-Semitism. Italians take that comment the same way—only in the context of *their* culture and society. Being a cross-breed, I took it both ways.

On reflection I think this young teacher had the best of intentions, had a program for us, and was trying to fit into a situation where she had to create respect and affection. But she didn't know us and had no insight into how we interpreted her words. She also didn't know that we talked to one another on the block after school; nor did she know that we were, in terms of performance, the top class at the school, and our parents, almost all of whom were working class, were proud of that and protective of our education.

One afternoon a number of us met and decided to destroy her ability to teach us and chase her out of the class and the school. We did the same crazy thing I experienced in classrooms where I taught over fifteen years later. We fell off our desks when we didn't stand on them, refused to do any work, hid all of the textbooks, set off sophisticated stink bombs and, in as many ways as our adolescent rebellion could imagine, made this poor woman's life miserable.

Naturally she called our parents to inform them of our behavior, and unfortunately she made the same mistakes with our parents that she did with us. Not one student in the class did not want to learn, but calling us "you people" with no respect for what we already knew or what our dreams or aspirations were was a sure formula for a short career in a school of strong children. And almost all children in their budding adolescence, no matter how they perform in school, are strong in ways many adults don't understand or don't want to acknowledge.

I remember her asking to see my mother and father and my grandparents. A whole bunch of parents from our class went to meet her, and she said, once again, "you people have disrespectful children."

Our parents, as a group, many of whom were experienced union organizers and political activists, went to the principal and said quite simply this teacher will not come back, as she does not honor or respect us. Our parents won but told us that, as students, we would have to show respect to the next teacher no matter what happened, because we had longer lives than junior high school.

My P.S. 82 experience has stood me very well, both in my own public school teaching and in my current work with beginning teachers. Going back to the teacher I observed who opened up her insecurities to her students and ended up with a class out of control, it is probably true that all white people in the United States take in racism with their oatmeal, but it is not true that all white people act based on racist sentiments. I also don't know whether the junior high teacher we wiped out was actually anti-Semitic.

It is essential, if you are going to teach in a community in which you are a stranger, an "other," not to air your guilt and uncertainty in ways that give children illegitimate authority. This is a complex social, philosophical, and political question. Overt racism simply cannot be tolerated. But white guilt, the anger some black teachers feel toward black students who are not performing, cultural confusion, and embarrassment are all part of teaching in America. And it is not just blacks and whites, but Latinos, Asians, East Europeans, and large-scale immigrations from Ireland, the Middle East, sub-Saharan Africa, Haiti, and the Dominican Republic as well as Native Americans that complicate the picture. Simple assumptions about who students are, what their experiences have been, and what their current conditions and motivations are all require "attunement." Teachers have to develop their listening skills and their talking skills now more than at any time I have personally known in education. How one speaks and how one hears are essential factors in how well one teaches.

Heraclitus said, "From things that differ come the fairest

attunement." It is a matter of translation, understanding, and strength. But in a major way it is also a matter of language, communication, and the creative arbitration of differences. Just recently I had to reattune myself. I had a lens-transplant operation; the lens in my right eye was extracted and replaced by a plastic lens. I had to learn to see again and reconstitute a world through new eyes. My organic eye and my plastic eye are learning to work together. It was more a brain problem than a vision problem. The challenge was to reconstruct the visual world and live in it—topsy-turvy in the sense that I had to see the world through new eyes and understand that the world could be turned upside down by something as simple as my eyes. The world didn't change. My vision did. I needed to integrate a changing visual sensibility. It was not a matter of going back to the way I used to see but of adjusting to a world somewhat familiar and thoroughly transformed. Quarters looked like nickels, apples seemed as small as grapes, and the redwoods around our house in Northern California got smaller. Topsy-turvies all the time and attunement all the time—opposites about how the world used to look and the way it looks now, but also the knowledge that it is the same world.

I am not a relativist—my eyes and my brain make my perceptions relative and require new integrations. The issue was how to react to these transformations. As it has turned out, it has been a revelation about the role of sight in the world and the amazing capacity of the brain to adjust to change. My eyes, in a metaphoric sense, were learning to reread the world with a new vocabulary.

The same readjustment applies in education, in particular to beginning teachers who are starting to see and talk from the other side of the desk for the first time. It is a question of keeping one's eyes in focus with the life around us. The way in which children feel they have to display themselves and speak in the classroom is essential to how they choose to perform in school. And the analysis and consciousness of your own language as a teacher is equally essential. How do you sound? How is anger expressed? Who is praised? How is failure expressed in front of the class? How are you exposed when you think you are failing, or perhaps even in despair? How many times a week do you express joy or thanks sincerely felt rather than mechanically administered as a matter of educational policy? Where is your joy in teaching, and how is that conveyed? To me, these are the essential questions teachers must confront, not the questions of test scores or covering the curriculum. Teachers should be as resistant and resilient as their students and learn the fine art of defying ignorant authority intelligently. After all, at its best, teaching is a nurturing and militant vocation and a wonderful thing to be doing in cynical times.

When you see trouble, attune your work and topsy-turvy your practice in the service of your students. Listen when you talk, and understand that, as well as talking to your students, you are being listened to. And laugh sometimes at the things you've said under pressure, and share that laughter with your students, and talk, talk, talk about how people speak and listen. We have to become a more literate society, and I think literacy will come not through testing and an obsession with standards, but through patient, intelligent, and sensitive speaking, reading, and listening.

Topsy-turvy thinking is not new. In 1710, Jonathan Swift wrote a short satire entitled "Meditation on a Broomstick" in which he said,

> a broomstick . . . is an emblem of a tree standing on its head; and
> pray what is man, but a topsyturvy creature, his animal faculties
> perpetually mounted on his rational, his head where his heels

117

should be, grovelling on the earth! and yet, with all his faults, he sets up to be universal reformer and corrector of abuses, a remover of grievances . . . and raises a mighty dust where there was none before.[26]

Teaching is a blessedly complex activity, which requires complex and continual attunement, and in which the upside down of topsy-turvy life in the classroom is one of the great joys and privileges of spending a life with children.

Part III

*Educational Reflections
on Becoming Sixty-five*

5.
Burning Out and Flaring Up

Even in Kyoto
hearing the cuckoo's cry
I long for Kyoto.
                                    —Bashō

On August 22, 2002, I celebrated my sixty-fifth birthday. Turning thirty, forty, and fifty didn't mean much to me. Sixty-five has made me reflective, especially since I am still teaching and working with young people and feel as if I'm just beginning to understand how children learn.

Recent work with students at the Center for Social Justice and Education at the University of San Francisco, however, and talking to them about the dialectic between teaching excitement and teacher burnout, reminded me of my first period of burnout and renewal. In 1964, after my first three years of teaching elementary school in Harlem, I became involved in community politics directed at improving the school where I taught, and directly confronted some of the racist policies that made it impossible for the children to learn. Most of the battles I fought were lost, and I learned how the New York City school system, with its resistance to change, was able to eject rebellious individuals efficiently and quietly by transferring them to new schools when they began to develop hopeful programs in their own.

This was the first of a number of times during my forty-five-year career as an educator when I found it necessary to withdraw for a while, regain energy, and learn something new myself. In particular, I decided to spend time teaching myself how to write, ultimately discovering and mastering my voice as a writer while realizing that I was also going to be a teacher. Teaching and writing have been at the center of my life since, and yet one of the most important times in my life was when I wasn't teaching and when my writing was terrible.

Homage to Catalonia

My wife, Judy, whom I had met during my first year of teaching, and I had saved a little bit of money and decided to head to southern France for a year. Riots were going on in Harlem, the parents and students we used to visit and socialize with after school and during the evenings were afraid to have us as guests, and I found myself returning with longing to a magical experience I had had a few years earlier, in the summer of 1959, after I graduated from college, when I had made a voyage of homage to hear the music of one of my great heroes, the cellist Pablo Casals. What I experienced at the Pablo Casals Festival in Prades in the South of France was one of the great lessons on teaching in my life.

Casals's playing, especially his rendering of Bach's cello sonatas, had provided the background for my writing and studying throughout college, and a tape of his performances accompanied me on my 1959 travels in Europe. What made them special for me was the combination of the passion of the music and Casals's humming, throaty voice that accompanied the sublime playing. Listening to the recordings, I felt that he was in the room with me.

While in Paris that first summer, I discovered that it was actually possible to hear Casals in person, see him rehearse, and be around musicians such as Victoria de Los Angeles, Jaime Laredo, and Mieczyslaw Horszowski. I promptly spent most of the money left for my stay in Europe on train fare to Prades, a hotel room in the city, and on tickets to all of the festival's concerts.

My "hotel" accommodations turned out to be a small room in a hayloft on a farm outside of town. When I arrived I was too tired to complain, and fell asleep with the door and window open. At sunrise I was awakened by a horrifying screech that gave me a cold sweat. I wasn't sure where I was and felt a longing for the Bronx, for friends or family, for a city, any city. It turned out to be a rooster crowing. I had never heard the sound before, and it had no resemblance to the soft *cock-a-doodle-do* in the books I'd read as a child. Instantly deciding that the farm wasn't for me, I walked to town and spent the money I had saved for a trip to Barcelona on the last available room at a pension hotel. The next morning I found myself at breakfast with the musicians who were also staying there, and I am still grateful to that rooster.

Casals was not at breakfast, but most of the other people in the dining room were either performers, their friends, or old-timers at the festival. I felt like a stranger at a family reunion. It was a delicious banquet of talk about music, gossip about the music world, and family gossip. There was a family feeling to Casals's world, which included not merely the musicians and their entourages but a small group of people who spoke a language I couldn't figure out and only later came to understand was Casals's native tongue, Catalan. These Catalan nationalists came to Prades, often by sneaking illegally across the border from Spain, to celebrate the culture and continue the struggle for democracy in Spain, where Franco was still in power.

For the rest of the festival, I spent mornings and afternoons at rehearsals, took a walk in the evenings, and went to the concerts at night. For lunch I explored the cafés and shops around the baroque church that was the main performance site. Breakfast and dinner were spent watching the performers who, after a few days, greeted me during meals and on the streets. I never had the courage to speak to any of them, and so I remained in the delicious position of full-time audience and learner during my whole stay at the festival.

During the rehearsals I had the opportunity to watch Casals as a conductor, a member of chamber groups, and a soloist. The music, in Casals's hands, was simple and passionate, reduced to blocks and elements that made space for great emotion. During the give-and-take of rehearsal, the talk was of nuances of feeling, of the tone and shape of transitions, and of the making of an effective, moving whole. I witnessed a community of learners, musicians enjoying one another's presence and teaching one another, learning from one another, and even during the occasional harsh exchange being clear that the purpose was the quality of the performance and not something egotistical or individualistic.

I had never been in such an educational setting with so much expertise and camaraderie. That time reached very deeply into me, reminding me that at the age of twelve I had wanted to be a public school teacher and help children in the way that these musicians helped and respected one another. The most precious thing I took with me from a year in Europe was the image of that community as a model of how people could come together and learn through common work. During the last performance of the festival, Victoria de Los Angeles, accompanied by Casals, sang Catalan songs arranged by

Casals himself. I cried with the rest of the audience, weeping not for the fate of Catalonia but for myself and the struggle to find a meaningful way to fill my life.

Casals at Prades became a model of how teaching and learning can happen in harmony and with grace, and I returned to that image during the years in New York when I learned how to be a good teacher. It became a standard for measuring the quality and tone of my own educational work. And the city of Prades was transformed in my imagination into a utopian vision of the ideal school community. I shared my dreams of Prades with friends and especially with Judy during my first years teaching in New York. So it was logical that when Judy and I decided to take a year off we headed for Prades in southern France, determined to spend a year living there. I went to teach myself the discipline of writing and to figure out how to be useful, over the long term, to the children, families, and community of P.S. 79, where I taught, and in the continuing civil rights and social struggles in the U.S.

In August 1964, a few days after the summer travel season ended and transatlantic fares on ocean liners went down, Judy and I left for Europe on the SS *Rotterdam*. After a short stay in Amsterdam and a longer one in Paris, we took a train to Prades by way of Perpignan. We left our luggage in the train station in Perpignan and, carrying a knapsack each, traveled on to Prades, where we hoped to find an apartment near the baroque church that was at the center of my Casals summer memories. I just about leaned out the window as the train approached Prades, trying to find the spires of the church and show Judy one of the coordinates of my dream city.

Instead of the spires, however, what loomed before us were tall, thin brick chimneys throwing black and brown smoke into the thick air of a small industrial city. My dream village had dissolved into the larger reality of the actual Prades I had ignored during my summer at the Casals festival, and I couldn't get off the train. Judy, as wonderful as ever, suggested we go on and see where we landed, so we paid the conductor to ride the train to the last stop, which was at a small French town called Bourg-Madame.

We got off in Bourg-Madame, which turned out to be a customs station on the Spanish border. There was nowhere to go from Bourg-Madame but through customs and on to Spain. So, headed for Casals's Prades, Judy and I found ourselves instead walking across the border into the place of Casals's longing, Catalonia, in Franco's Spain.

The first town across the border is Puigcerdá, in the middle of which remains the burned-out shell of a Catholic church destroyed by the Republicans and anarchists in 1936 during the Spanish Civil War. It had not been rebuilt, and stood—quite explicitly, as we later found out—as a reminder that although Franco continued in power, the will of the Catalan people was not broken.

Judy and I hadn't planned to spend a year in Spain under the rule of Franco, yet that evening in Puigcerdá we felt comfortable and welcome in the midst of Catalonia in the midst of Spain, surrounded by people who spoke Catalan and French but no Castilian Spanish. In addition, on a purely selfish level, we found Spain inexpensive enough that our anxiety at being able to afford a year in Europe immediately disappeared. We spent one night in a hotel in Puigcerdá, and the next day set off down the road in search of a place to settle. We didn't need any maps; we had no idea where we were going. That moment of freedom made me feel like singing out and thanking whatever spirit there was that allowed me to be with someone I loved on a quest that was all hope and renewal.

Judy and I set out on the road leading away from the border and into Spain, and after a while came upon some people gathered at a bus stop. We joined them and bought tickets on the first bus that came along to the last stop on its line. We boarded the bus and began to look for a place to settle, a small town that would somehow approximate my dreams of Prades. Halfway through the trip we came to a small, terraced village, Martinet, built on a hillside. It immediately felt right to both of us, so when we reached the end of the line, we took the next bus back and got off at Martinet. We wandered around, and it was right—a place where, at that moment in our lives, we could live and work. As it turned out, if not by fate then by wonderful and benign serendipity, there was a new house at the very top of the town that had never been inhabited and might be for rent. Judy and I spent the night in the hotel in Martinet, and then the next evening crossed the French border and walked several miles to the farmhouse, where the owner of the house lived. After a long conversation in halting French, he agreed to rent the house to us for sixteen dollars a month for one year. In addition, he agreed to provide a *matrimonio*—a wedding bed—for us, and a chest of drawers for our clothes. The house had no other furniture beyond a woodstove, and our new neighbors advised us to go to the local carpenter and have some made. It was a way of our becoming a part of the local economy, one that turned out to have the unexpected bonus of introducing me to the carpenter's father, an anarchist who had fought in the Spanish Civil War, who later became my mentor and guide.

It took a while, but after a few weeks we slowed down from the pace of our life in New York. I had hoped to buy time during this year, and there it was: all day, every day, to write—with no excuses. I forced myself to develop daily writing rituals (ones that I have used for over forty years and forty books while continuing to teach).

In Martinet, the quality of sound and silence was completely different from New York's noise. In the country, small sounds ring clear and true through the silence, and the smallest sound distracted me when I began to force myself to write in Martinet: the bus or a truck down the road (very few cars passed through), a rooster crowing, the sounds of the pigs next door, or the sheep on their way to pasture. I began to play music while I wrote, and found that the right music surrounded and protected me so that I could write without distraction. The music I could find was a thirty-three-minute record of Spanish *zarzuelas* (light operas), which I played over and over every morning while writing. It set a constant, familiar sound environment for my work. I found myself wrapped inside of my writing; though the writing itself wasn't particularly good, the event of writing was enough of a delight to keep me going through clumsiness and anxiety.

The first thing I tried was a fictionalized narrative of my childhood in the southwest Bronx during the 1930s and '40s. This first and longest work of that year was perhaps one of the least successful "growing up Jewish in the Bronx" novels ever attempted, though recently I've rewritten parts of that effort into my essay "The Tattooed Man." My students in Harlem were also very much on my mind, and I attempted to convey some of their despair and pain through short stories and theater pieces. My student Robby, and Peter (a student at P.S. 79 who was not in my class but whose life Judy and I had become involved with) became the dual foci of my writing.

That year, I developed the habit of working on many writing projects at the same time; I'm sure the model for that way of working came from my father, who was a building contractor always simultaneously finishing a project, estimating new projects, in the middle of several jobs, and working with subcontractors before beginning a new job. Some of his jobs were big and took over a year to complete; others were as small as installing a bathroom or changing the display and sales space in a shoe store. I realize now that I work obsessively, like my father—only my jobs are written, not built.

The first of two serious writing projects began then concentrated on Robby and her family. The senseless killing of one of her older brothers and the pain she and her mother endured were unlike anything I had ever known personally. This was my first experience of a promising young person dying prematurely on the streets, and I felt outraged—aggrieved but also angry at my previous innocence. It afforded my first direct, non-classroom insight into the effects of poverty, pervasive violence, and demoralization on family life. My working-class neighborhood in the Bronx had had a few gangs and occasional rumbles, and some kids I knew got stabbed or beaten up. We all knew about violence within some of the families on the block and were aware of the violence in the larger world—the violence of the poverty our parents had suffered during the Depression, of union struggles, of World War II and the Holocaust. But this was tempered by optimism about the economy and by the security that, at least for now, the war was not in our community, on our streets, and in our apartments. We didn't have to cover our backs every time we went out, or worry every day about whether someone would return safely from a simple trip to the corner store.

However, in the early 1960s, teaching at P.S. 79 and visiting with my students' parents, I learned that there was a war in the community that has not ended to this day. I don't believe that "war" is too strong a word to describe the constant fear and anxiety all of my students lived with daily. The feeling of living within a community under siege that many of my students expressed in their classroom writing was palpable. We could talk about it, dream about changing things, propose specific small projects to make things better, or figure out how some individuals could save themselves. But to point to a single enemy that could be confronted, or to analyze the cause of the community's continuing decay, was hopelessly difficult. Certainly racism was a major factor—many of the people who lived in the neighborhood had come up from the segregated South only to face job discrimination and out-and-out racism in the North. They found themselves unwelcome below Ninety-sixth Street, squeezed into ghettos no less isolated and impoverished than Eastern European shtetls. Because the community was overwhelmingly black and Puerto Rican, the white people who created and perpetuated the ghettos were not present except in the forms of cops, teachers, and social workers. People fought one another, and sold drugs to one another, trying to find ways to take a share of the community's inadequate pot of money. Though there were some successful families and a few coherent communities and neighborhoods as well as a growing sense of political militancy developing in the community, almost everything was set up for self-destruction. Since there was no "other" to strike out against, all of the negatives in the community were turned inward. Rage was always just a bit beneath the surface for everyone, and any person could explode at any given moment if something broke through their tight mechanisms of rage control.

To me, Robby and her family represented good, sensitive, caring, intelligent people caught on the edge despite their best efforts. My understanding of Robby's brother's death was that he had kicked a heroin addiction and refused to get reinvolved with some of his former friends. But he knew too much, and somehow they did him in. Neither Robby nor her mom gave me the specifics. His death was, to them and to me, an irretrievable loss, an insult to the very idea of hope that they had nurtured so carefully and in such difficult circumstances. During the school year, amidst all of the rest of the turmoil, Judy and I had a number of conversations with Robby. Despite her barely controlled rage, she had determined not to give up and was fighting her mother's despair. It was that battle and the absolute loss of her brother that I tried to write about.

I wanted to make people hurt the way Robby did, to help them understand the strength and agony of her mother, and the sheer waste of her brother's life. It wasn't clear to me what form the telling of the story should take. I hoped to shout out, to engage people in a way they would not forget. In Martinet, it was possible for me to think through how to redeem something out of their pain and move people to confront the fact that people like Robby were the victims of an internal, silent, but national war against people of color and the poor.

The idea of shouting out took hold of me, and it seemed logical to try to write the script of an opera where people could actually shout and cry and sing out. I love Italian opera and, in Martinet, far away from anyone who could tell me what I couldn't do or shouldn't attempt, I decided to try an opera. And, going back to my love of Greek culture, at the very time I began to think beyond it in my teaching and encountered Afrocentric curriculum for the first time, I decided to use the form and shape of Greek tragedy and write a blues opera in one act. In retrospect, this seems a way I was trying to merge cultural forms that seemed to me to be equally powerful.

The blues opera *Robby* was the first writing I had ever done about my students that wasn't an assignment for some college class or a formal report to a school authority. In it, I tried to portray Robby as she was: not as a student but as a person, one of whose identities is "student." This writing reflected the way my thinking about children had evolved through my teaching. I learned that unless you knew and cared about your students outside of the classroom, about their strengths, dreams, and aspirations as well as their problems, you could easily limit what they could do as students and miss the opportunity to develop a learning community where they could act as themselves and not according to some image they had developed of how children should or shouldn't behave in school. I came to understand that the ability of children to act naturally and at ease with themselves, their friends, and teachers within a learning environment is the key to effective education.

Throughout my year in Catalonia I found myself thinking about the children not in the context of school, but in the larger context of their lives outside of school—their cultures, religions, families, and histories. Freed from the everyday concerns of organizing and managing a classroom, I also began to rethink what education might be, and therefore what school might look like, if we kept in mind the children at their best, in their dreams, and with people they love. I had never encountered a child who did not have some corner of her or his life where they were learners and lovers—that is, where they stole time to feel in connection with their selves and the world. Hardly ever was this schooltime, however, and it seemed to me that learning outside of school was a rich and underexplored place to experiment with new models of education.

Thinking and writing about Peter was just as troubling and difficult as were my concerns with Robby, though I now see all of the writing I did that year as moving toward discovering my written voice and preparing me to attempt *36 Children*.

Peter, who was eleven at the time I met him, lived next door to one of the children in my class. He and his mother were invited to one of the dinners we had with students and their parents. He was a lonely and very quiet child who always smiled. Sometimes the smile seemed sly and knowing. Other times it was distant, almost unconscious. Those times, Peter appeared to be away somewhere inside of his head. Those moments, he didn't respond when you spoke to him, and his mother told me that there were times when you had to shake him to get his attention.

He lived in the midst of chaos and disorder. The one-bedroom apartment he shared with his mother, brother, and four sisters was dominated by a TV. Spread out in front of the TV were blankets where the children often ate, watched, and slept. There was no space for him to do anything but dream.

Peter's teacher took a particular dislike to him and made his life miserable. I often let him sit in my room to read or do a craft project and protect him from daily tirades and abuse. His silence and perpetual smile drove his teacher, who was having a hard time controlling the class anyway, crazy. It was no use to protest to the administration, which treated tenure as more sacred than educational responsibility, so I did the best I could in the circumstances.

One night Peter's mother called Judy and me at home and begged us to come over and help her with Peter. She said he had gone berserk, tried to stab his younger brother, drew monster faces on the TV screen, and tried to break it by slamming it to the ground. She said she had called around and there was no hospital willing to take him. She didn't want to call the police, who would treat him like a criminal and not someone who was disturbed.

Judy and I drove uptown and saw Peter. He was sitting on the floor, smiling as usual—only this smile was wicked and triumphant. He was talking to some imaginary companion he said had encouraged him to kill the TV. There was a large steak knife on the floor next to him and, even in the midst of the usual disorder, we could tell that he had been on a rampage. His sisters and brother were huddled in a corner, obviously terrified.

When we came in, Peter greeted us as if nothing had happened, and I suggested that he and his mother come with us.

After making a few calls we discovered that the only place that would admit and care for him was the emergency psychiatric ward at Bellevue Hospital, so we drove down there. The people at Bellevue were marvelous. A nurse and orderly came out, and he immediately went with them. A few minutes later the nurse emerged and said he wanted to talk to me. I went in to see him and, to my astonishment, I had never seen Peter looking better. His smile was genuine and open. He thanked me for taking him there, and when I asked him if he wanted to go home, he said, no, it was nicer in the hospital. He had managed to escape through madness, real or feigned, and was happy for the breathing space the episode had provided him.

I talked with Peter over the next few months and even corresponded with him from Martinet. Indeed, the treatment he got at Bellevue and then, when he was released, from the Big Brother he was assigned and who became like a father to him for years, helped him take control of his life. As a consequence of his explosion, his mother was moved into a three-bedroom apartment she had been waiting for for at least two years, and he was sent to a new school, where he had a teacher who cared about her students.

Peter was on my mind—the logic to his outburst and the way in which the educational and medical system could have contributed to his misery but instead had actually helped him. I tried to figure out what was going on in his mind, to imagine the conversations he had with his imaginary companions, conversations I am convinced were going on in school as well as at home. And I tried to understand his outburst and collapse as a move to sanity, as a cry for help rather than as a sign of disintegration.

My six months teaching at the Reece School in Manhattan for schizophrenic children had taught me that there was a logic and coherence to the worlds of schizophrenic children, and it was this coherence that I tried to convey in a short story about that incident, which was very hard for me since I had never attempted any fiction before. I did finish the story and, upon rereading it, see the difficulties I had as a writer. The story seems dead and incoherent. There was no convincing voice in the writing, and the ending shows that I did not fully understand Peter or know where to go with the narrative. For me this was another important lesson in learning how to write with a convincing voice and to think about children's lives.

Sharing the worst as well as the best of my work with Judy has been essential to my growth and development. Being able to talk freely about children and schooling, politics, personalities—anything—and knowing that our relationship would never be at stake no matter how strongly we disagreed or saw the world differently has provided me with a stable center from which all of my writing and teaching has grown.

In Martinet I was able, for the first time, to reflect upon the lives of my children as an educator rather than as a teacher. As a teacher I was concerned with daily life in the classroom, the rituals of community, the weather and its effect upon the children, their progress in math and reading that week and month. There was no time to reflect upon the larger educational issues of how children learn, how schools enhance or inhibit learning, how different content areas are best approached, and how the differing cultures, personalities, and skills the children bring to the learning situation affect their learning.

During that year I also corresponded with about half a dozen of my former P.S. 103 students. Their letters were often troubling. Junior high was difficult, there were troubles on the streets, and despite a few academic and personal successes, the racial climate in New York City was tense, and the children (now no longer children but young adolescents) were bewildered about their futures. I felt guilty about my happiness in

Martinet, about my being able to buy slow time to grow when they were consumed by the fast and hostile time of life in their community. However, I stuck with my commitment to writing, forcing myself to develop the discipline and skill to be able to write well enough to influence the way people thought and acted. I felt this opportunity might never come again, so I held to it tenaciously. We didn't return to New York until our year was over, and even then we were tempted to stay in Catalonia for another year.

In addition, in the early spring I became the student of an old man whose name I never learned. He chose me as a pupil because we had two unplanted terraces in front of our house. One afternoon he came up to our house and began speaking to me in Catalan, not bothering to find out whether I understood him. He beckoned me follow him, and we went into the lower of the terraces where he picked up some soil and then pointed to neighboring terraces where people had turned the earth in preparation for planting. Then he said something I understood across languages, which was in effect that in a poor community that feeds itself, it is wrong to leave unplanted terraces. Then he left, beckoning for me to wait, and returned with two shovels. He put one down and, with the other, began to turn the soil. I stood watching, angry that he was trying to force me to do something against my will, yet intrigued by the adventure of following his lead and learning how to garden Martinet-style. The only planting I had ever done in my life was in a Victory Garden outside of my elementary school during World War II, with the teacher yelling at us to hurry up and not telling us what seeds we were putting in the ground or what to look for as things grew. It was a thoroughly unpleasant experience.

The Anarchist, as I'll call him, was bent over, and his face was wrinkled and windblown from years of smuggling cigarettes over the Pyrenees from Andorra to Martinet and then passing them on to people who sold them on the streets in Barcelona. During the months when we put in the two terraces and nurtured the garden, I gathered some stories about his life by listening carefully, calling on my French, and trying to flow with what he said without straining to understand every word. He was the father of the carpenter who had made our furniture and knew a lot more about Judy and me than we would ever know of him.

I learned that he was an anarchist, both philosophically and in his everyday life. He was due an old-age pension but did not collect it since he refused to give his name to any authority. In fact, he did not recognize the legitimacy of governmental authority of any sort, and so was not officially alive in Spain.

One day when it was time to plant beans he motioned for me to follow him, and we walked to the top of the hill and then over into a wooded area and through to a swamp. There, he cut poles telling me that they would grow back and that no wood that could be used for building would be wasted on the garden. He went on, as he grabbed a vine and bundled the poles, telling an animated story that I struggled to understand but that eluded me. I knew he was trying to teach me something, but I just couldn't get it. He then placed one bundle on my shoulder and showed me how to adjust it so that it didn't feel heavy, and then picked up the remaining three bundles himself and we went back to our terraces.

My rituals with the Anarchist lasted until we left Martinet. He showed me what were weeds and what were plants, tricks of getting water to the plants from our well, and plants and birds that I hadn't noticed. It was as if I had assumed an apprenticeship in listening and looking, a welcome silencing of my dependence upon words rather than perceptions. I believe this short time he shared with me has had a major effect on my growth as an educator and as a person. It was the beginning of a more conscious effort to look and listen without judging, to slow down and take advantage of what is revealed in the pauses and silences in relationships as well as what is said or acted out.

As June approached, Judy and I had to decide what to do for the next year. New York, the children, teaching, the everyday lives of the people in the community around P.S. 79 were very much on our minds, and the responsibility for rejoining the civil and social struggles in the United States provided compelling reasons for us to return. There was no moral excuse not to return to the U.S., so we did, arriving in New York in August 1965. I didn't have the slightest idea how I would pick up where I had left off, and was confused about the kind of role I could play to help the children and the community. But, against all of my apprehensions, we were welcomed back. There was work to be done, and the children were still there. I have found that there are times when you need relief from the struggles, and times when you return with enhanced energy and can be more effective. However, the privilege of leaving and becoming renewed is not open to the communities I serve of young people who are poor. I do the best I can, but I understand that I am privileged. And I know that at this point in our country's sad and hypocritical story there is no will or strategy to eliminate neglect, lack of learning resources, and benign malevolence on the part of the people in corporate and government leadership. However, as a 1968 poster from France hanging on our kitchen wall proclaims, *La Lutte Continue*—"The Struggle Goes On." As I try to tell my current students, who often get burned out and tired, a lifetime of struggle is not a bad thing, and needing to see decency prevail in your time is a call, not a promise. It is a call to act for justice and equity in the schools, but not a promise of success. Persistence and renewal are necessary.

Appendix

of special interest to educators

Developing Teachers for Social Justice: A Report on an Attempt to Keep the Struggle for Social Justice Alive in the Schools

OVER ONE QUARTER of all public school teachers in the United States will retire in the next decade. This can provide a great opportunity for the development of energized, young teachers who, as future leaders, might revitalize public education and redefine progressive education according to current needs and struggles. Or, as in California, it can be used as an excuse to mold a new teaching profession that knows only increasingly parsed standards, high-stakes testing, rigidly structured Eurocentric curriculum, English-only learning, and a highly controlled, punitive, banking-system education.

In California, through directives, legislation, and the redefinition of teacher-credential programs, the very words "bilingual education" will be formally eliminated from the vocabulary of schooling, replaced by "English-language learning." Bilingual classes will abandon the use of first-language teaching, and students will be taught and tested in English only. Phonics is already the religion of the early grades, and multiculturalism is back in its place as "holiday celebration time." There will be no more bilingual education credentials, and teacher education students themselves will be subject to high-stakes tests on phonics, English language learning, lists of standards, and even rigid forms of classroom management. A major aspect of controlling public education is being shaped by the increased demands by states on departments of teacher education. The boundary between teaching students and testing students is becoming increasingly unclear, and the performance gap is increasing. Many people already teaching are demoralized. In addition, the far right is engaged in an assault on the very enterprise of public education. The small schools movement, a ray of hope in a slough of despond, is struggling along.

Any radical teacher-education program in the State of California at this time has to consider the tension between developing critical, perceptive, skilled, and motivated new activist teachers, and the grim realities and struggles they will likely face while working in poor urban public schools. When I was asked by the dean of education at the University of San Francisco to develop and direct a teacher-education program, these realities were clear to me. It made sense to develop a program that was focused explicitly on issues of social justice as they relate to life in the school, one that would acknowledge the standards movement and comply with minimal state requirements but would shape the content of learning in a creative and progressive way. This implied, at the least, developing antiracist curriculum, working through what can be called the problem of "teaching other people's children," and confronting the damaging aspects of high-stakes testing. It also meant helping student teachers develop the concrete skills that would enable them to teach to very high standards while they developed material that respected the knowledge and experiences of the students and the school's community. And finally it implied preparing, as much as possible, for them to be working against the grain and to be willing to see themselves as agents of change and organizers.

Fortunately, the administration at the University of San Francisco, a Jesuit university, with a commitment to infusing issues of social justice into all of its programs, welcomed the program. It is very unlikely that any state-supported institution of higher education in California would have touched it.

The Center for Teaching Excellence and Social Justice is now going into its third year. We had a cohort of twenty credential and master's degree students the first year, twenty-five the second year, and twenty-seven the third year. The cohort stays together for a good part of the program and does outside-of-class educational projects together. One of the goals is to develop each cohort as a learning community and a peer-support group. I hope that the students will see one another as comrades fighting similar battles, though likely in different schools. I also hope this sense of common struggle will extend beyond the students' time in the program and will become a mutual support and organizing group through their teaching careers. This has succeeded beyond my expectations. The reason, I believe, is that, unexpectedly, 90 percent of the students who entered the program already had from one to six years' teaching experience in Bay Area urban schools and were looking for such a community of learner-teachers to support their work. Coming into a teacher-education program with other students facing the same struggles they were already having in the classroom creates a strong bond among the students that energizes the whole program.

The development of the center within the context of a teacher education department that was initially indifferent, at best (we are now, after three years, more fully and comfortably integrated), was a major challenge. I was very fortunate in having an assistant, Mike Sahakian, who has become central to the operation of the organization and to the continual contact with students that has become characteristic of our work. Developing a program is not a one-person job, and it is as crucial to build an infrastructure for the support of students as it is to develop the student cohorts.

Initially recruiting students was a problem, as it was agreed that the center would not dip into the pool of students normally recruited by the University of San Francisco School of Education. In addition to that restriction, I decided to recruit students who had already manifested a commitment to social justice and provide a place for them to hone their ideas and develop practical skills that would enhance that commitment. The criteria used were not rigid, and our first group of students was involved in issues of social justice that ranged from environmental activism to youth media, community arts, and anti-racist work. Others, who were already teaching, manifested their concern for social justice in the work they did in the classroom, and a few of the students had studied critical theory in college with an eye toward acting for social justice. The common theme running through all of the students' applications was the desire for a more just world and a willingness to act to make it a reality through work with children.

I lost sleep and visited schools and programs in the quest for students. In the course of one of my school visits, a third grader asked me what I was doing and I told her, "pounding the pavement" for students. She asked me what I was pounding it with, and I almost said, "with my head."

My first student came to me from the radio. I was listening to a call-in show, and one of the callers had asked about teacher-education programs that dealt with social justice. I called the station and left my name and the name of our program. Within a day I got a call back, held an interview, and had a student. He has just finished his credential program and is currently teaching in the San Francisco Unified School District. He is also an active member of Teachers for Change and Teachers for Social Justice.

I also recruited several Teach for America veterans who decided to stay in teaching and struggle to reform public education after their original commitment was over. I have reservations about Teach for America and its emphasis on teaching as social service rather than as professional commitment. However, the students who entered teaching through Teach for America and applied to the center's program had survived teaching in underserved urban schools for several years and remained committed to making public education work. I continue to recruit from this pool and have found wonderful young people who are potentially great teachers.

Friends held house parties throughout the Bay Area for young people they knew who wanted or needed teaching credentials. People who entered the program recruited their friends and colleagues, and some people who had read my work also joined in recruiting. What began as a seemingly futile quest for students became organic and somewhat self-directing. What surprised me most about the approximately twenty-five students was that with all but a few exceptions, everyone was currently teaching on an emergency credential and had substantial experience.

Now entering our fourth year, we do practically no recruiting. Most of our students come through word of mouth from former students, which is the greatest compliment we can have for the effectiveness of the program. In addition, there are a number of other people who teach in the center's program.

Student-teaching placements and supervision are done

from within the center, though our students take some of the same classes as students from the other teacher-education options at the School of Education. One class in particular is the early literacy class, which focuses on phonics and other early reading methods mandated by the State of California.

My desire to shape the program implied that, at least for the first few years, I would teach as much as the university would allow and, within the guidelines of the state, be able to shape the content of these classes. The first challenges I faced were to develop a creative program that had a distinct identity while aligning itself to California standards, which in my view have become rigid and somewhat absurd. However, nothing prevented us from analyzing this absurdity and looking at ways to work within the system while working toward changing it.

The design of the classes was a challenge, since the center's students were overwhelmingly practicing teachers and had very different experiences, perceptions, concerns, and questions than students who enter education programs straight from college. In a way, they were young colleagues of mine who had embarked on the same educational journey that I have been on all of my adult life. Therefore, the most important goals were to marry theory and practice in all of the classes, to allow for their questions and concerns, and to build the cohort.

For the first two years, the program was built around two required classes that met for two and a half hours each on consecutive days. One was formally titled Philosophical Foundations of Education; the other, Psychology of Education. I taught these back-to-back classes and tried to weave a number of themes back and forth across the classes, illustrating how philosophical and psychological issues related to one another and to the specific challenges of shaping teaching for social justice. One of the key texts was Nathan Huggins's "The Deforming Mirror of Truth," which allowed both of the classes to focus on constructing narratives and on the critical analysis of educational and philosophical theories of childhood, learning, and schooling. We also made extensive use of the ideas of Paolo Freire, Myles Horton, and Lev Vygotsky, among others.

My orientation comes more from Myles Horton's work at the Highlander Research and Education Center in New Market, Tennessee, than it does from the work of Paolo Freire. Highlander and Myles's work is not as popularly known as Freire's. However, Highlander has been engaged in major struggles for justice in the United States since 1932 and has been a central force in the early Congress of Industrial Organizations workers' democracy movement, the civil rights movement, the environmental justice movement in Appalachia, and the struggle for poor people and workers' rights. Over the years Highlander has been a gathering place for poor and working people. It was the only integrated, Southern residential facility throughout the '30s, '40s, and '50s. Its goal was to help people educate themselves and develop movements for social change. People such as Rosa Parks, Eleanor Roosevelt, Septima Clarke, Ella Baker, Pete Seeger, Martin Luther King Jr., and Woody Guthrie all passed through Highlander and participated in its educational workshops.

Myles, one of the founders of Highlander, was a mentor of mine from 1977 until he died in 1990, and my wife, Judy, and I had the privilege of working with Myles on his autobiography, *The Long Haul* (NY: Teachers College Press, 1998). Central to Myles's thinking and Highlander's work is the idea that the people who have a problem are the ones who own the solution to the problem. What I believe he meant by that is that knowledge of the specific nature of a problem, the strengths and weaknesses of the opposition and of one's own community, resides within the community itself. His belief in the intelligence and ingenuity of people, no matter how they are oppressed, focused his work on the articulation and maximizing of people's strengths. Freire's work is much more expert driven, involving people who teach at universities and who also work within communities and codify their experiences for them or with them. My translation of Myles's thinking to work within schools was to emphasize listening, understanding children's ideas and thinking, and fundamentally respecting the intelligence of the students and their capacity to help you teach them.

Freire's notion of codification is also something we utilize in the program as it lends itself to visual representation, theater, and other forms of group expression. A codification is a representation of a problem within a community that can be presented to a group as a basis for critical discussion and the development of an action plan. For example, here's part of a simple codification, drawn from one of the main texts we use, *Training for Transformation*, 3 volumes, by Anne Hope and Sally Timmel (Harare, Zimbabwe: Mambo Press, 1984, available in the United States from the Grailville Art & Bookstore, Loveland, OH 45140; 513-683-0202), which is the most detailed and useful exposition of the application of Paolo Freire's work I have encountered.

Two people perform this playlet. One comes on with a great big grin and an open heart and mind. This actor wears traditional dress and has a false right hand hidden in the sleeve of his or her shirt. He (or she) opens her hand to shake the hand of a second actor who comes on stage wearing European clothes. The European welcomes the handshake and then rips the hand out of the other actor's shirt and goes off smiling. A discussion of the effects of welcoming the Europeans ensues.

During the first year, in addition to Freire, Horton, and *Training for Transformation*, we used the work of Lisa Delpit on the dilemmas of teaching African American children using progressive education ideas developed in white middle-class liberal schools in the first half of the twentieth century. We also used Louise Dehrman-Sparks and Carol Brunson Phillips's *Teaching/Learning Anti-Racism* to help our students develop antiracist programs in their classrooms.

The idea of centering the class this way was to introduce ideas of democratic education and critical and cultural analyses that lent themselves to the transformation of the students' current classroom practice. My idea was that this material would provide students with critical tools and the techniques of transforming ideas into teaching materials and strategies. Many of the assignments involved actually developing and testing what we were discussing in class within the students' own classrooms. Sharing the results of such work was very effective in developing ties among students in each cohort as they saw one another as creative workers working toward common goals.

To give a more specific idea of how the classes worked, the following are excerpts from the syllabus, with some explanations and some of the assignments. The syllabi themselves are formatted in a traditional way, as is the class schedule of the whole program. We are aligned to the California state–mandated curriculum in order to provide students with California teaching credentials. However, within the context of a rather benign-looking structure, there is an enormous amount of freedom to shape the content and the structure of the program in a way that manifests its commitment to democratic education and creative pedagogy. The pedagogy is creative in that it evolves each year but it does not adhere rigidly to any standard version of critical pedagogy, Freire-based learning, or progressive education. We utilize all of them but are situational. That is, the program is formed with the intention of helping students understand their own creative role in drawing from many radical democratic traditions, their own experiences, and the voices from within the communities they serve in order to make an effective and excellent education for their students.

Introduction to the Idea of Philosophy as Narrative

Discussion of narrative and of alternative perceptions of events and ideas, such as the diverse views and understandings students are likely to encounter in their classrooms.

Analyze Plato's "Allegory of the Cave" as an example of an attempt to create a master philosophical narrative. Read Huggins, Nathan I., "The Deforming Mirror of Truth," from *Revelations* (New York: Oxford, 1995), pp. 252–83.

Paper: Choose an event and describe it through different narrative frames. Pay attention to the deformations that occur when stories are told and identified as absolute truth. Also discuss the power of narrative to confirm or deny social justice.

The Highlander Idea

1. Myles Horton and the relationship between theory and practice in education.
2. The philosophy of listening and learning from others.
3. Community resource mapping.
4. Learning from the students you work with and the community you work in. Explicating the phenomenological and existential approach to understanding and social justice.
5. Maxine Greene and the ontological role of authenticity and choice. The role of the teacher as philosopher and creator of educational theories.
6. Aesthetic philosophy and the role of the social imagination in learning.

Texts: Greene, Maxine, *Teacher as Stranger* (Belmont, CA: Wadsworth, 1973), pp. 3–25, 267–302.

Horton, Myles, with Judith Kohl and Herbert Kohl, *The Long Haul* (New York: Teachers College Press, 1998).

Videos: Bill Moyers interview with Myles Horton, *You Gotta Move: A History of the Highlander Center.*

Paper: Develop a community map of a place you work in or know. Also, project that map into alternative visions of organizing communities based on discussions of the social imagination.

Problem-Posing Education

Introduction to Paolo Freire and class discussion. Participatory activity in the development of codifications.

Texts: Brown, Cynthia, *Literacy in 30 Hours: Paolo Freire's Process in North East Brazil* (Chicago: Alternative Schools Network, 1978).

hooks, bell, *Teaching to Transgress* (New York: Routledge, 1994), pp. 45–58.

Hope, Anne, and Sally Timmel, *Training for Transformation* (Harare, Zimbabwe: Mambo Press, 1984).

Kohl, Herbert, *Paolo Freire: Towards the Splendid City* (Milwaukee: Rethinking Schools, 1998).

Paper: Develop a codification for the school or child-related organization you work with or have worked with in the past. Develop exercises to use that codification in practice to examine and act upon a social issue in the school or in the classroom.

Children as Philosophers

1. The philosophical thinking of children.
2. Introduction and class discussion of questioning and how young people's philosophical questions can be integrated into curriculum and class discussion.
3. The role of powerful ideas in understanding the philosophic foundations of education.

> Texts: Matthews, Gareth, *Philosophy and The Young Child* (Cambridge: Harvard University Press, 1980).
> Wesker, Arnold, *Words as Definitions of Experience* (London: Writers and Readers Publishing Collective, 1976).
>
> Paper: Describe some of the philosophical questions that you raised as a child, heard children raise, or have pondered yourself, and create a dialogue about one of them. Also, develop a lesson on a philosophical issue that you can teach by using a list of significant ideas according to Wesker's model.

Social Justice Education

1. An overview of the history and philosophy of education from the perspective of social justice.

2. Discussions of the applications of philosophical ideas to the transformation of educational practice.
3. Creation of social justice–focused lessons in small groups within the class.

> Text: Ayers, William, Jean Ann Hunt, and Therese Quinn, eds., *Teaching for Social Justice.*

Observing Children

1. Overview of the theories of growth, development, and learning that we will be considering.
2. Class discussion of Center students' current views about how children learn.
3. Lecture with examples of ways of observing children when they are engaged in learning.

> Texts: Hawkins, Frances Pockman, *"The Eye of the Beholder."* (Boulder, CO: Mountain View Center for Environmental Education, 1976).
> Korczak, Janos, "Why Do I Clear Tables?" from *Ghetto Diary* (New York: Holocaust Library, 1978).
>
> Paper: Write reflections on how you learned to read. Try to do an imaginative re-creation of the times and places, and make them come alive for the reader.

Sham, Vulnerability, and the Social Aspects of Learning

1. Examination of the way in which sociological concepts like sham, social performance, humiliation, and vulner-

ability can enrich classroom observation and transform classroom practice.

2. Consider refusal to learn and resistance to learning as well as ways of overcoming them.
3. Focus on how to write about children and learning.

Texts: Henry, Jules, *On Sham, Vulnerability and Other Forms of Self-Destruction* (New York: Vintage, 1973).
Kohl, Herbert, *"I Won't Learn from You"* (New York: The New Press, 1994).

Paper: Describe how you see humiliation or conscious refusal to learn work in your classroom or schools. Be specific—do a case history.

Other Teachers

1. Examine the role of culture, class, and race in human development.
2. Consider ways that teachers can observe themselves or other teachers using strategies similar to those used for observing children.
3. Discuss issue of how teachers learn.

Texts: Delpit, Lisa, "Skills and Other Dilemmas of a Progressive Black Educator," from *Other People's Children* (New York: The New Press, 1995), pp. 11–20.
Delpit, Lisa, "The Silenced Dialogue," ibid., pp. 21–47.

Paper: Describe racial and cultural relations among teachers and administrators at your school.

This is a sample of what is central to our programs.* There are other classes and student-teaching seminars as well (fortunately, our students are able to do most of their student teaching in their own classrooms while visiting other classrooms and getting support from master's degree teachers who are chosen because of their teaching excellence and experience working for social justice).

One of the goals of the program is to expose students to experienced people whose work in education and social justice has been effective. We have had a number of people work with the students. Among them are Arnold Perkins, currently director of Health and Human Services for Alameda County and former director of the Koshland Program of the San Francisco Foundation. Perkins talked to the students about issues of race, health, and the interface of the school with social services and communities. He also consulted on the question of developing alliances among schools, health professionals, community-based organizations, and foundations.

Another guest of the Center for Teaching Excellence and Social Justice was Betty Halpern, former director of the Early Childhood Program at Sonoma State College and current professor emeritus at Sonoma State. She discussed the history and philosophy of progressive education with the students and consulted on how to develop curriculum that had a significant social justice component. We have been able to persuade Dr. Halpern to teach in the program as an adjunct.

A third guest was Gary Delgado, director of the Applied Research Center in Berkeley, and one of the founders of the

---

*For a copy of the complete syllabus of the class, please contact Mike Sahakian at the Center for Teaching Excellence and Social Justice, 2130 Fulton Street, San Francisco, CA 94117-1071.

Center for Third World Organizing. He demonstrated the School Report Card, which is used as an assessment of racial relationships at a school. Mr. Delgado has agreed to continue to work with the Center as we develop a curriculum that has as a central focus issues of social justice.

At the end of the spring semester 2003, we had a series of conversations with Joseph Featherstone on the future of progressive education, and a daylong workshop with Dolores Huerta on education and activism. The latter was held jointly with TEAMS, the School of Education's AmeriCorps program. In addition, we had a seminar with Sonia Nieto on bilingual education and the role of families in education.

Several student initiatives will contribute to the further development of the Center. One of the students, a former Silicon Valley computer specialist and currently the computer specialist at Thurgood Marshall High School, set up a listserve for the entire class. Throughout the semester, students have been communicating with one another on class readings and on the educational problems they face in their own classrooms. They have also shared ideas for class projects and papers and have become continual collaborators.

In addition, several students set up a Sunday study group to discuss the class readings and reflect on class discussions. I also have run a series of seminars on weekends on theater and writing. Participation is totally voluntary but has been continual and, according to the students, quite rewarding. The students have made arrangements to visit one another's classes. This is neither for credit nor required, but comes out of their passion for teaching and learning from one another.

At present, our students are involved in setting up discussion and organizing groups with their peers in the public schools, and a group of students is discussing setting up a small school within the Oakland Unified School District.

Each semester has culminated with the students' development and presentation of educational games, theatrical performances, CDs, murals, quilts, and other artistic representations of their individual and collective journeys taken in our learning community. We also have a residential weekend in Point Arena, California, where I have developed an education library, learning center, mini-Highlander at my home. The retreat has no fixed agenda and every educational agenda imaginable. It is a chance for the cohort to spend social time together and reflect upon their learning and their current work in the schools. It also provides an opportunity to plan ways of keeping the cohort together after the students graduate. The goal is to develop a peer support group when the students are teaching and not in school.

The central aim of all of this is to have teachers work with their hearts, their minds, their eyes, hands, and ears as they shape an education adequate to the brilliance and promise of their students. This is particularly important in the schools the students work in—in Richmond, Oakland, East Palo Alto, and San Francisco, where the need for energetic, caring, moral students is a desperate matter.

Teaching under stress and acting to create situations that are free of teacher-proof programs, cynical and racist prohibitions that suppress students' home languages and cultures, and institutional resentment of students who are considered failures is difficult enough for the experienced teacher. Without peer support, a strong will, and clear convictions, plus a large bag of tricks, thoughtful pedagogy, and an abiding love for children, young teachers can hardly survive. I sometimes feel uneasy supporting my students as they embark on a life of struggle, but they tell me not to worry. They remind me of myself and other friends who, after forty years of activism in education, continue to confront the beast in the service of the children and their communities. These young teachers' intelligence, passion, and energy and their new ways of defining problems and developing solutions continue the struggle for justice in education in ways that inspire us older folk. There's nothing wrong with being a troublemaker in a troubled world.

This is just a preliminary report on a work in progress. I find energy and renewal in the presence, commitment, and work of my students—a welcomed antidote to the despair over the future of public education that overcomes me at moments.

Notes

1. Friedrich von Schiller, *Joan of Arc,* Act 3, Scene 5

2. Jules Henry, "Education for Stupidity," *New York Review of Books* (May 9, 1968, vol. 10 no. 9)

3. "Close Up: Joe DiMaggio," *Life* magazine (May 1, 1939), p. 62

4. *New York Times* (August 23, 2002), p. 1

5. Franz Kafka, *The Castle* (New York: Schocken, 1998), pp. 57–58

6. Oscar Wilde, *The Picture of Dorian Gray* (1891)

7. Jules Henry, *On Sham, Vulnerability and Other Forms of Self-Destruction* (New York: Vintage Books, 1973), p. 120

8. Ibid.

9. Maxine Greene, *Releasing the Imagination* (San Francisco: Jossey-Bass, 1995), p. 35

10. Jules Henry, "Education for Stupidity"

11. *Yiddish Proverbs,* ed. Hanan J. Ayalti (New York: Schocken, 1949), p. 25

12. David Hilbert, "Mathematical Problems," *Notices of the American Mathematical Society* (August 2000, vol. 47, no. 7)

13. Thomas Nagel, *The Possibility of Altruism* (Princeton, NJ: Princeton Paperbacks, 1978)

14. Ernst Bloch, *The Principle of Hope,* 3 volumes (Cambridge, MA: MIT Press, 1986)

15. David Hilbert, "Mathematical Problems"

16. Walt Whitman, *Leaves of Grass* (1891)

17. Kornei Chukovsky, *From Two to Five* (Berkeley, CA: University of California Press, 1968), p. 118–21

18. Ibid.

19. Gerald Robert Vizenor, *Interior Landscapes: Autobiographical Myths and Metaphors* (Minneapolis: University of Minnesota Press, 1990), p. 73

20. Virginia Hamilton, *The People Could Fly* (New York: Knopf, 1993)

21. Faith Ringgold, *Tar Beach* (New York: Crown, 1991)

22. Howard Gardner, *The Mind's New Science* (New York: Basic Books, 1985), p. 6

23. Eduardo Galeano, *The Book of Embraces* (New York: W. W. Norton, 1992), p. 121

24. *Generation* magazine no longer exists and every effort has been made to find a copy and to trace the teacher.

25. William Blake, from *The Illustrated Poets: William Blake* (New York: Oxford University Press, 1986), p. 38

26. Jonathan Swift, "Meditation on a Broomstick," from *A Modest Proposal and Other Satiritical Works* (New York: Dover Thrift Editions, 1996), p. 24